D1094676

THE
UNIVERSE
VERSE

written & illustrated by James Lu Dunbar

THE
UNIVERSE
VERSE

James & Kenneth Publishers
Berkeley, CA

THE UNIVERSE VERSE
Copyright © 2013 by James Lu Dunbar
All rights reserved
www.JLDunbar.com

James & Kenneth Publishers
2140 Shattuck Avenue #2406, Berkeley, CA 94704
www.JamesAndKenneth.com

First edition, 2014

Printed in China
through Four Colour Print Group, LLC
in Louisville, KY

Photo Sources:
Patrick J. Lynch & Carl Jaffe, MD, eye on cover;
National Aeronautics and Space Administration, all other photos

Publisher's Cataloging-In-Publication Data
(Prepared by The Donohue Group, Inc.)

Dunbar, James Lu, 1983-
    The universe verse / written & illustrated by James Lu Dunbar. -- 1st ed.

    p. : ill. ; cm.

    Summary: This rhyming comic book explains the scientific concepts surrounding the origin of the
universe, life on Earth, and the human race, from the Big Bang to the scientific method.
    Interest age level: 10 years and up.
    ISBN: 978-1-888047-25-7

    1. Cosmology--Juvenile literature. 2. Life--Origin--Juvenile literature. 3. Human beings--Juvenile
literature. 4. Science--Juvenile literature. 5. Cosmology. 6. Life--Origin. 7. Human beings. 8. Science.
9. Comic books, strips, etc. I. Title.

QB983 .D86 2014
523.1   2013919396

This is for my baby.

Special thanks to my partner, Trina.

And to all of my parents,
particularly my Mom and Dad.

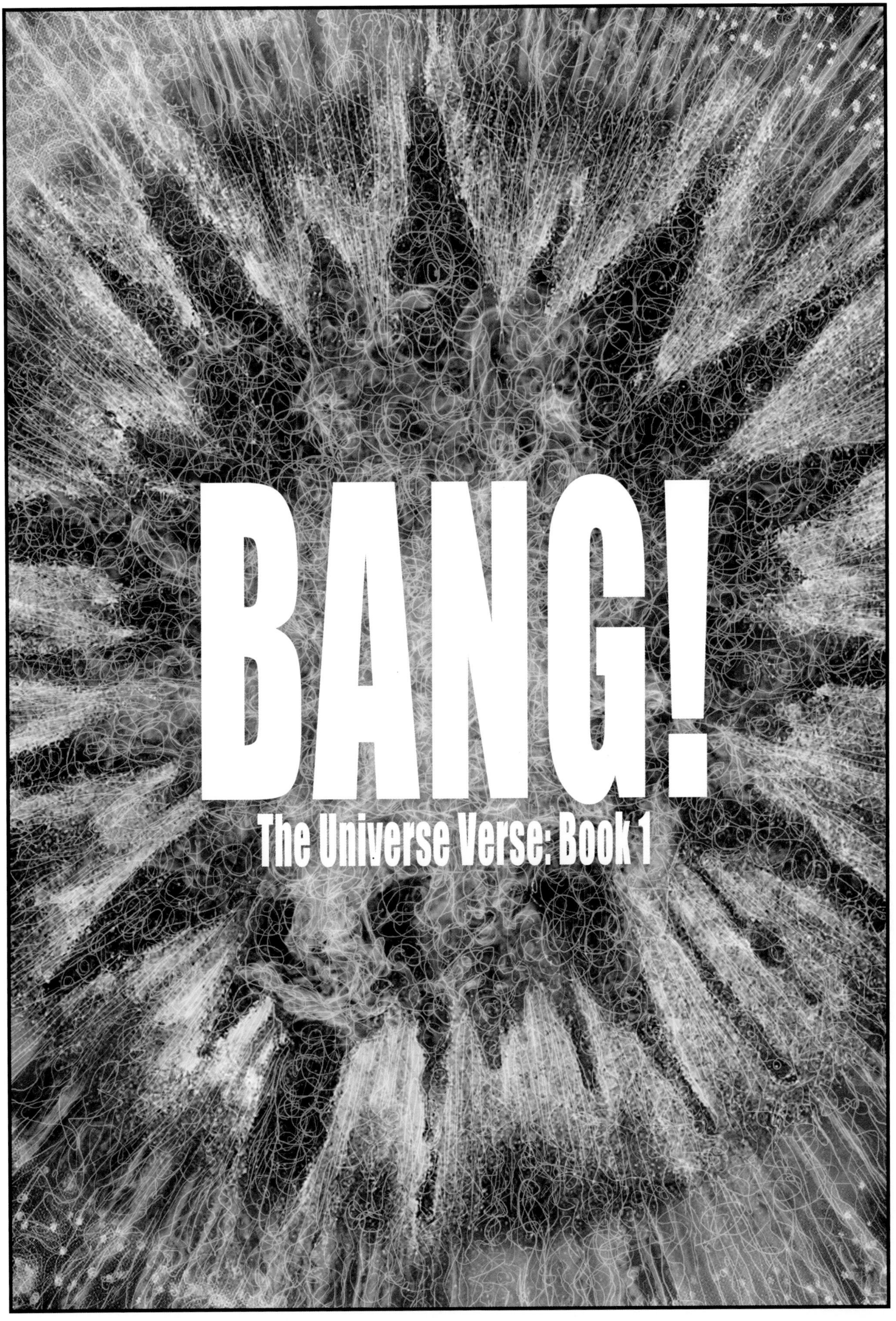
BANG!
The Universe Verse: Book 1

The universe is full of magical things
patiently waiting for our wits to grow sharper.

-Eden Phillpotts

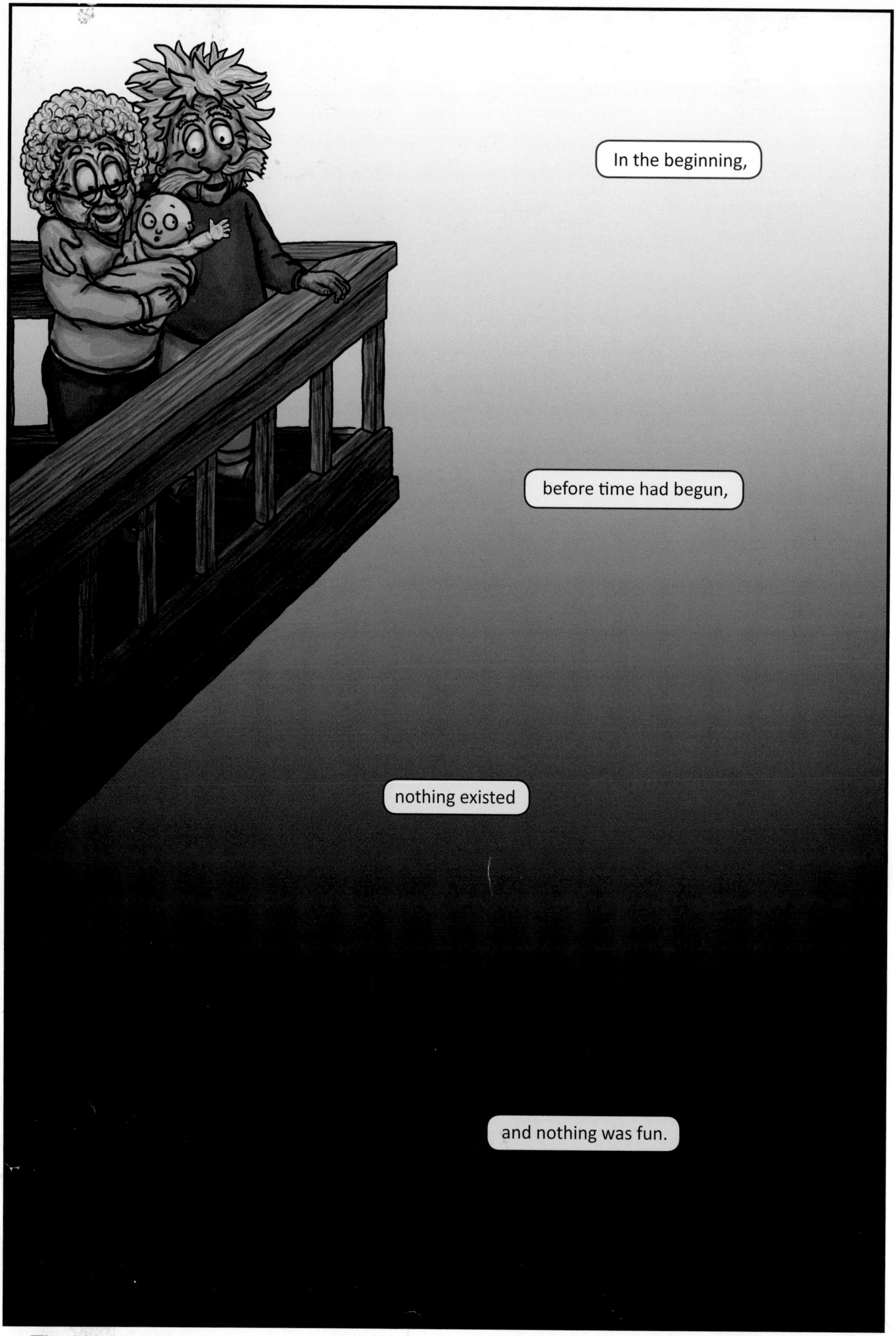
In the beginning,
before time had begun,
nothing existed
and nothing was fun.

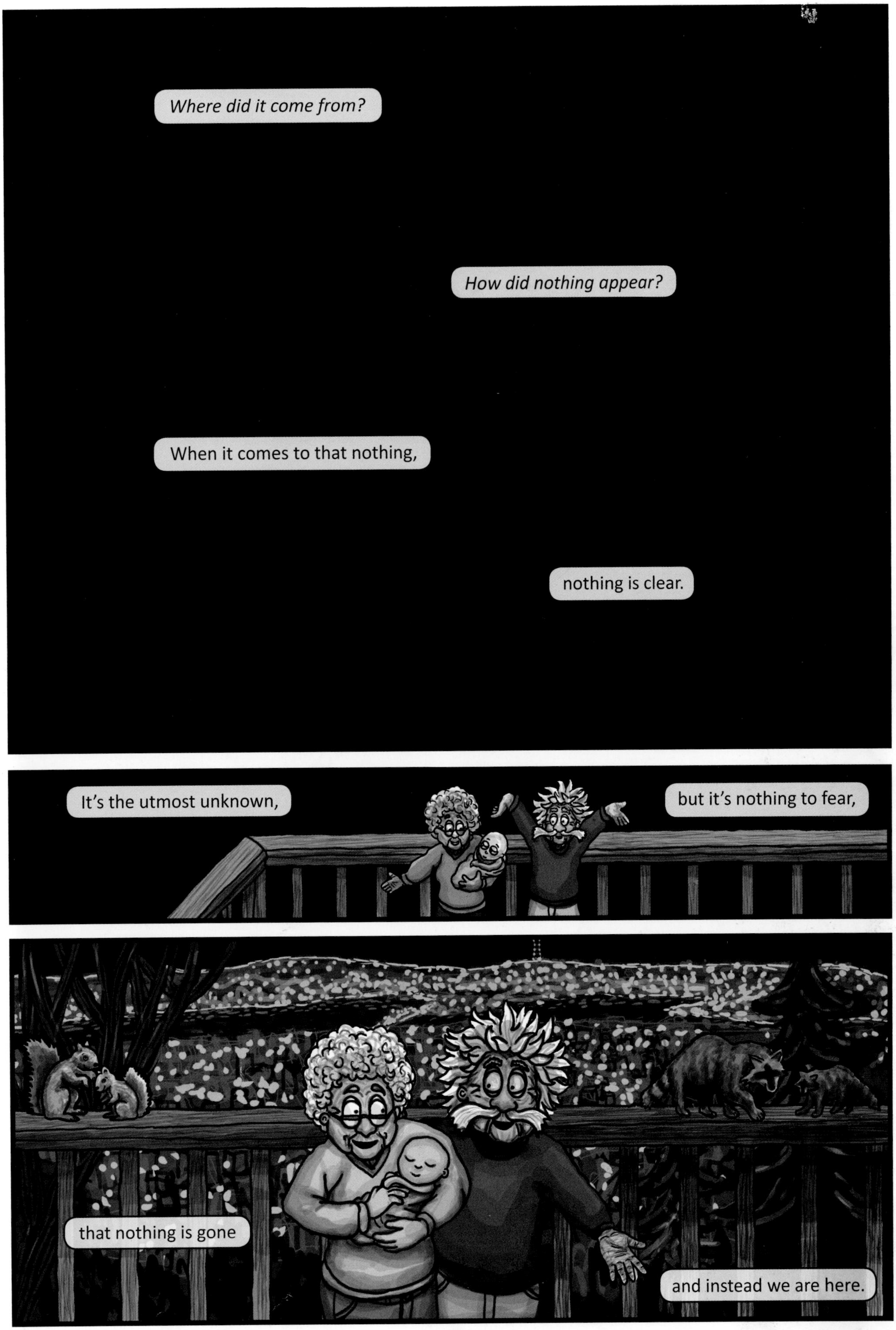
Where did it come from?
How did nothing appear?
When it comes to that nothing,
nothing is clear.
It's the utmost unknown,
but it's nothing to fear,
that nothing is gone
and instead we are here.

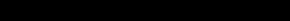

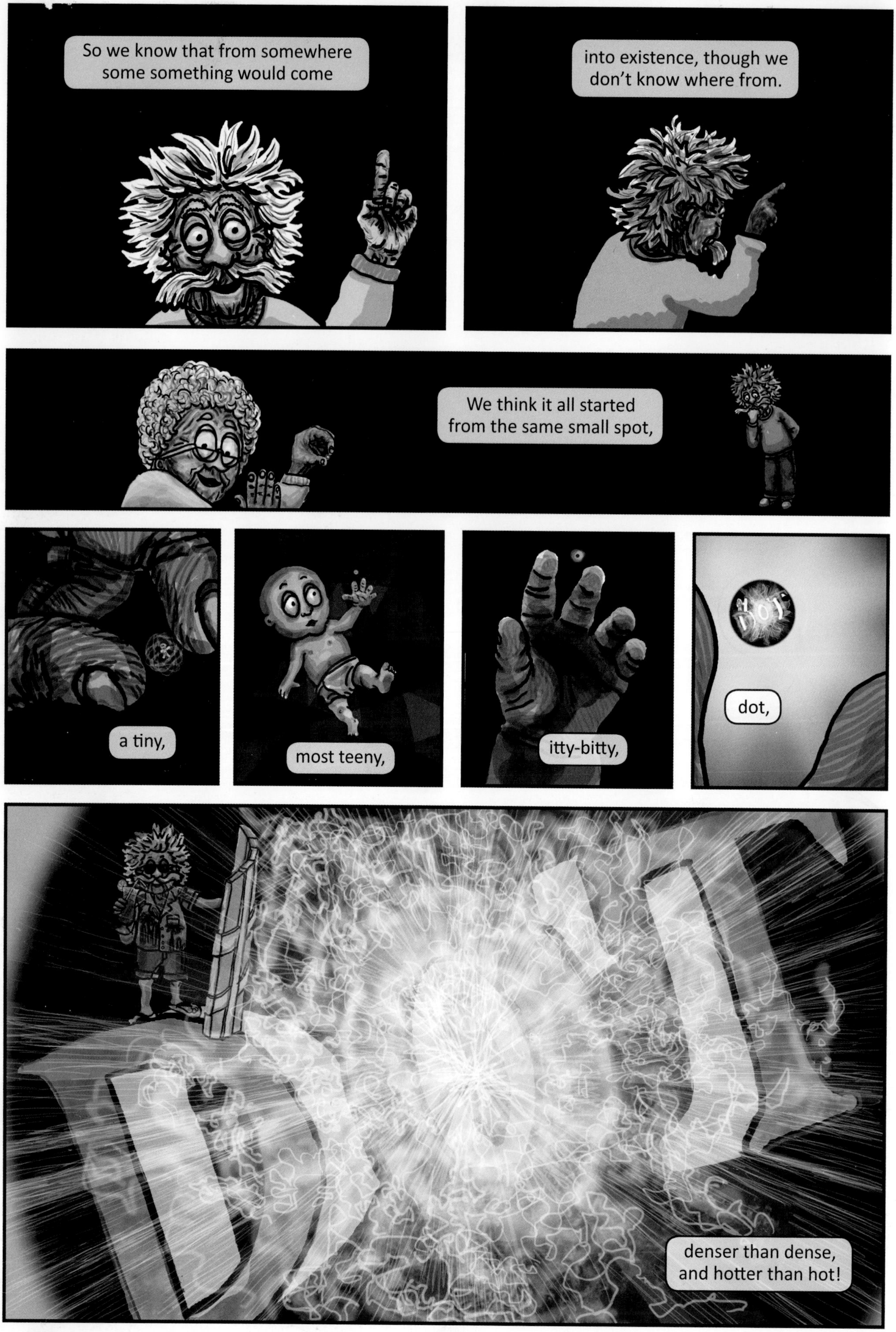
So we know that from somewhere some something would come
into existence, though we don't know where from.
We think it all started from the same small spot,
a tiny,
most teeny,
itty-bitty,
dot,
denser than dense, and hotter than hot!

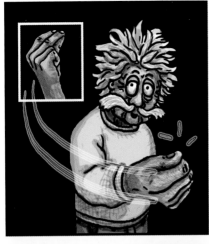

Then lickety-split, things got going fast.

That dense little dot did not get to last.

With a *Bang!*,

and a *Boom!*,

and a most massive blast,

in every direction

existence was cast.

James Lu Dunbar

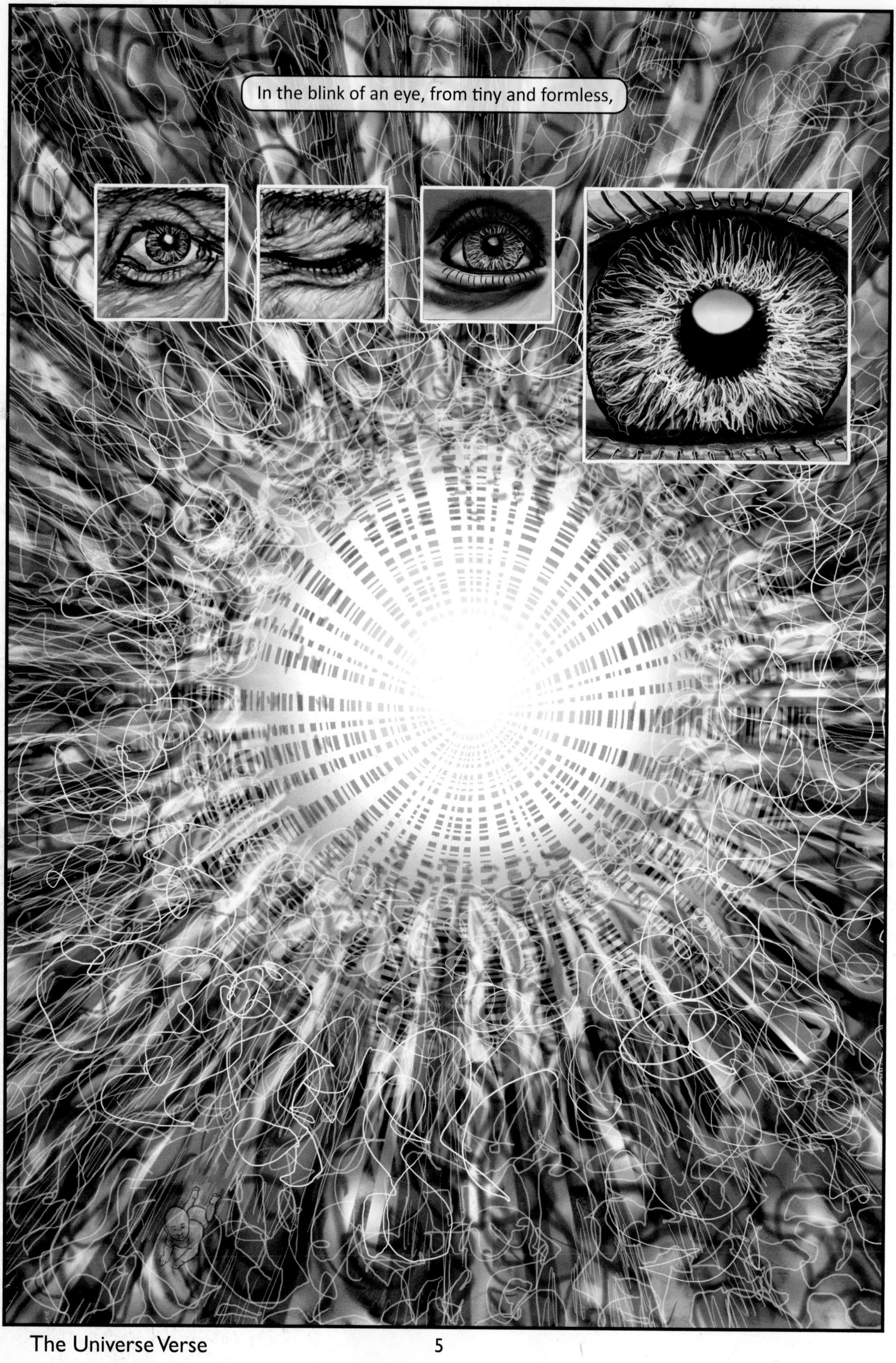
In the blink of an eye, from tiny and formless,

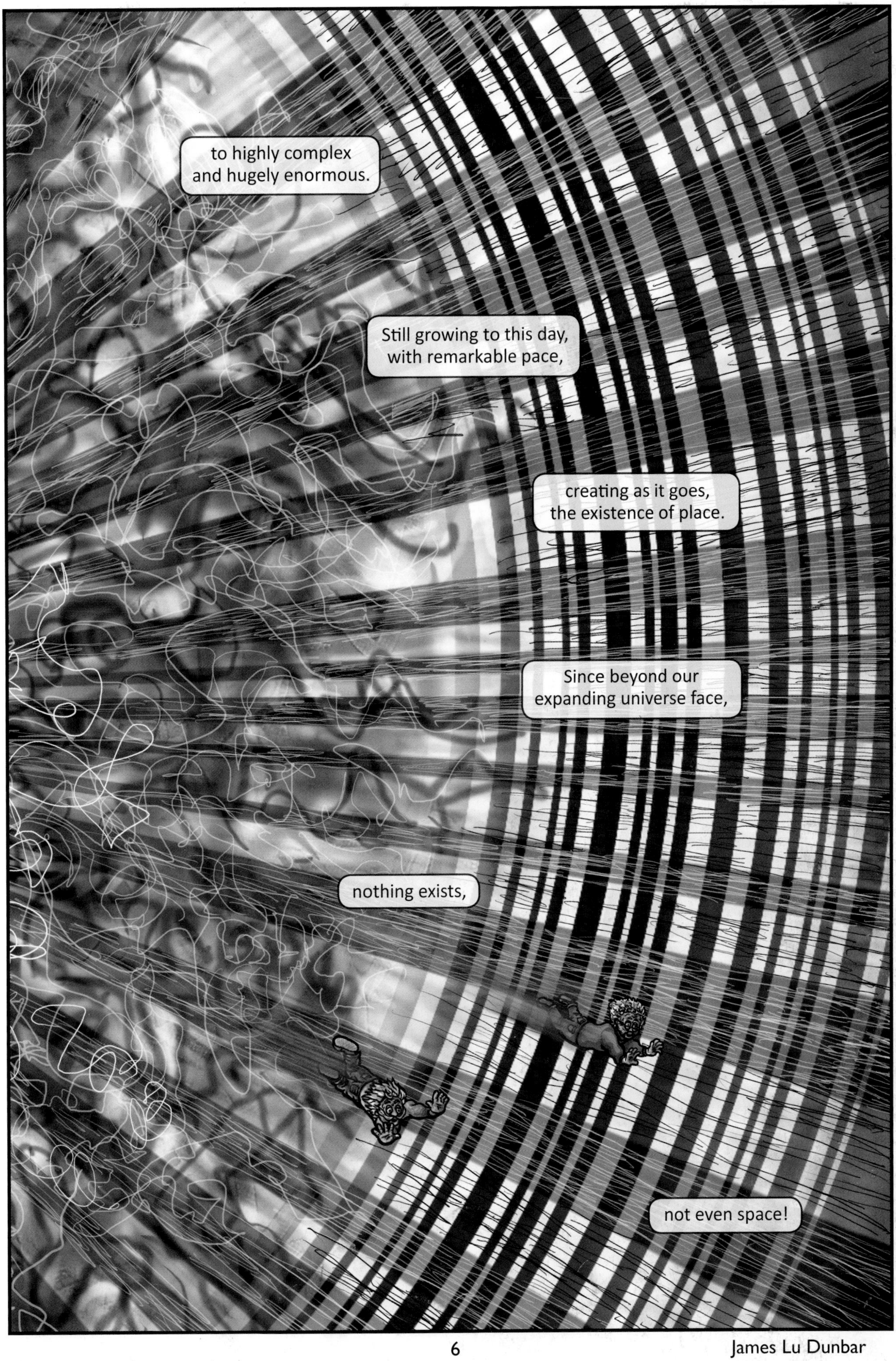
to highly complex
and hugely enormous.
Still growing to this day,
with remarkable pace,
creating as it goes,
the existence of place.
Since beyond our
expanding universe face,
nothing exists,
not even space!

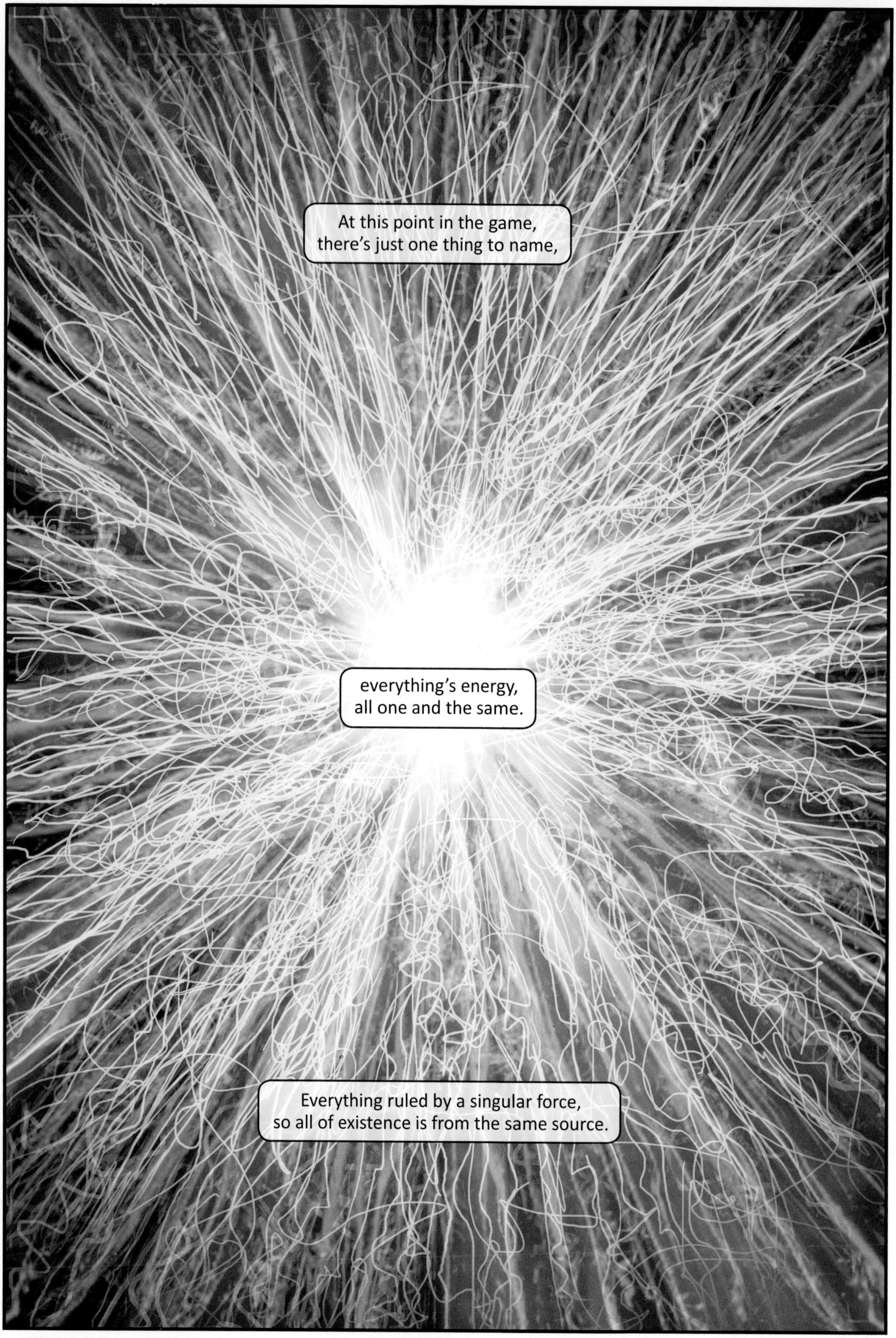
At this point in the game,
there's just one thing to name,
everything's energy,
all one and the same.
Everything ruled by a singular force,
so all of existence is from the same source.

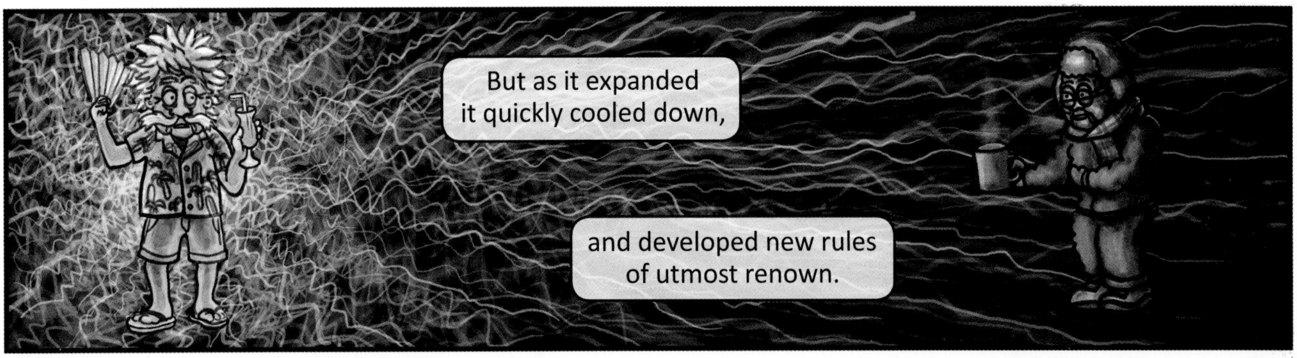
But as it expanded it quickly cooled down,
and developed new rules of utmost renown.

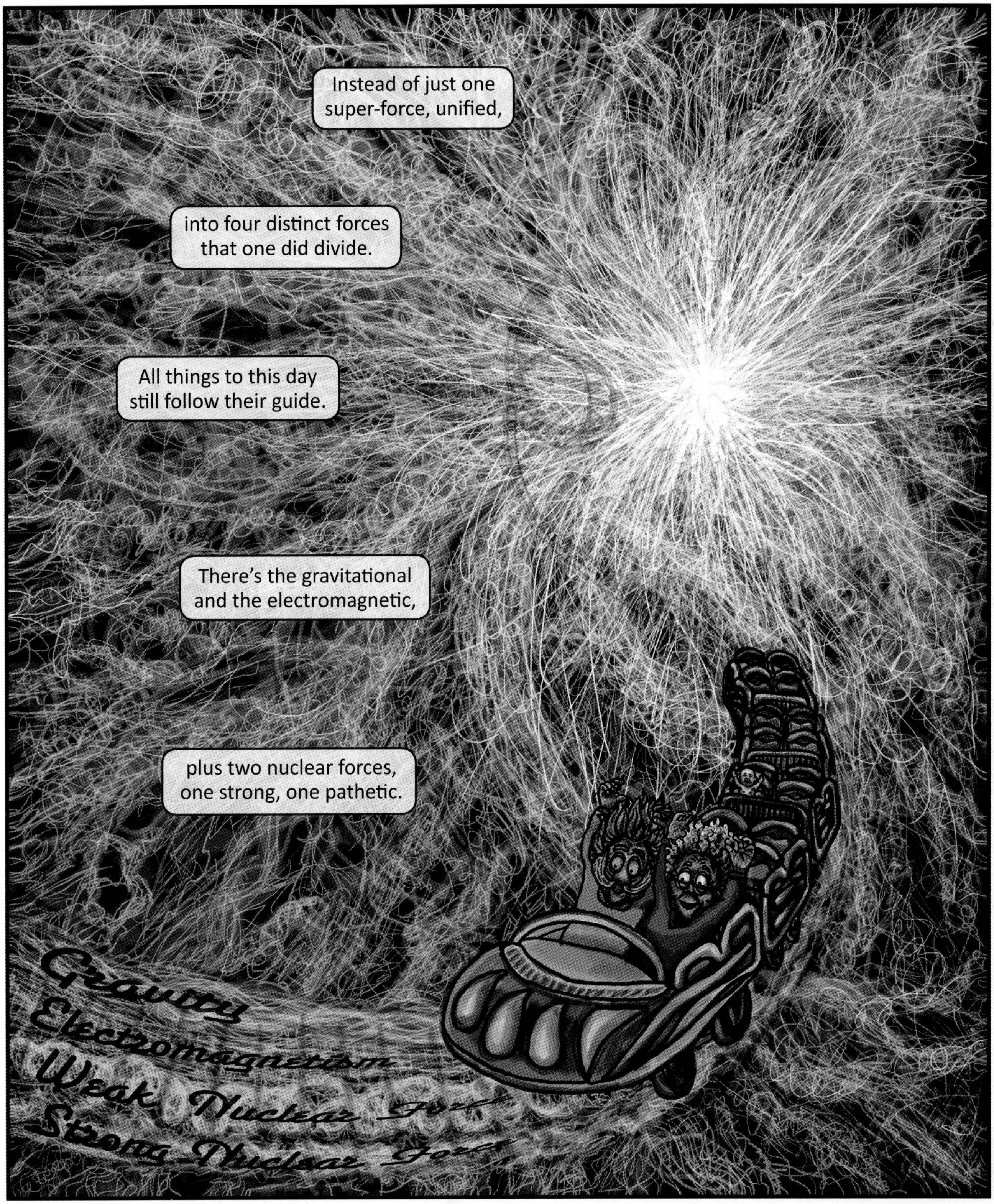
Instead of just one super-force, unified,
into four distinct forces that one did divide.
All things to this day still follow their guide.
There's the gravitational and the electromagnetic,
plus two nuclear forces, one strong, one pathetic.
Gravity
Electromagnetism
Weak Nuclear
Strong Nuclear

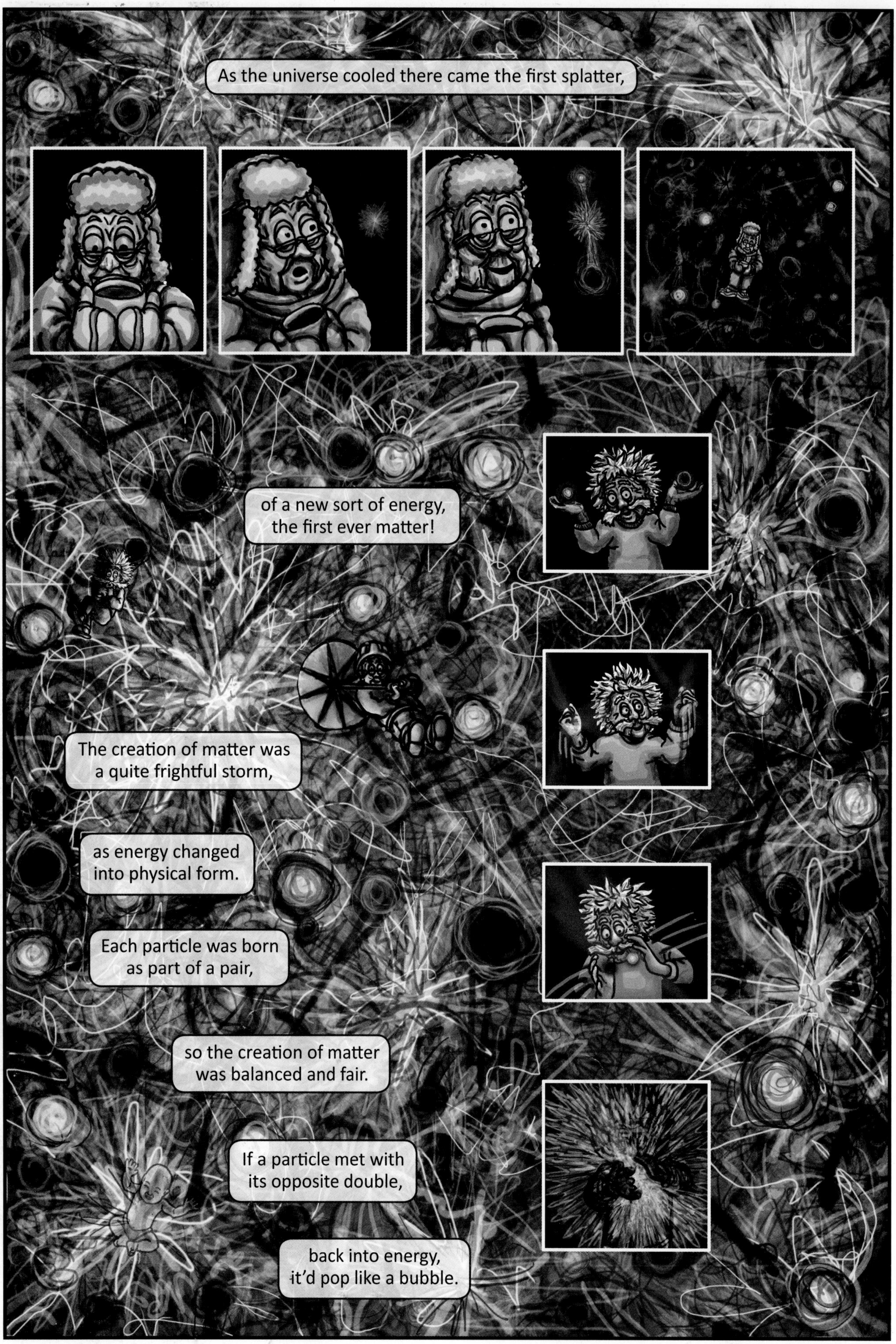
As the universe cooled there came the first splatter,
of a new sort of energy, the first ever matter!
The creation of matter was a quite frightful storm,
as energy changed into physical form.
Each particle was born as part of a pair,
so the creation of matter was balanced and fair.
If a particle met with its opposite double,
back into energy, it'd pop like a bubble.

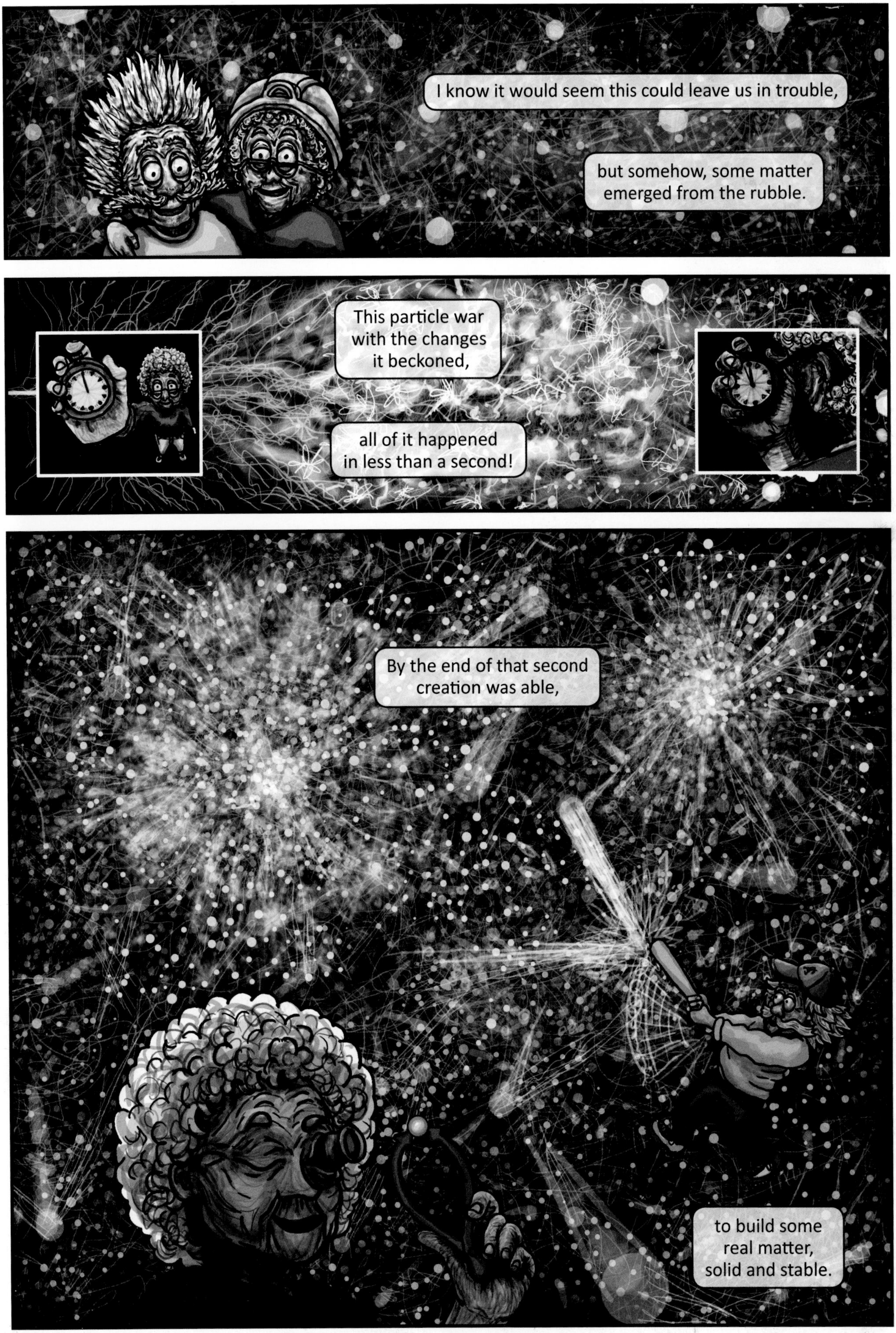
I know it would seem this could leave us in trouble,
but somehow, some matter emerged from the rubble.
This particle war with the changes it beckoned,
all of it happened in less than a second!
By the end of that second creation was able,
to build some real matter, solid and stable.

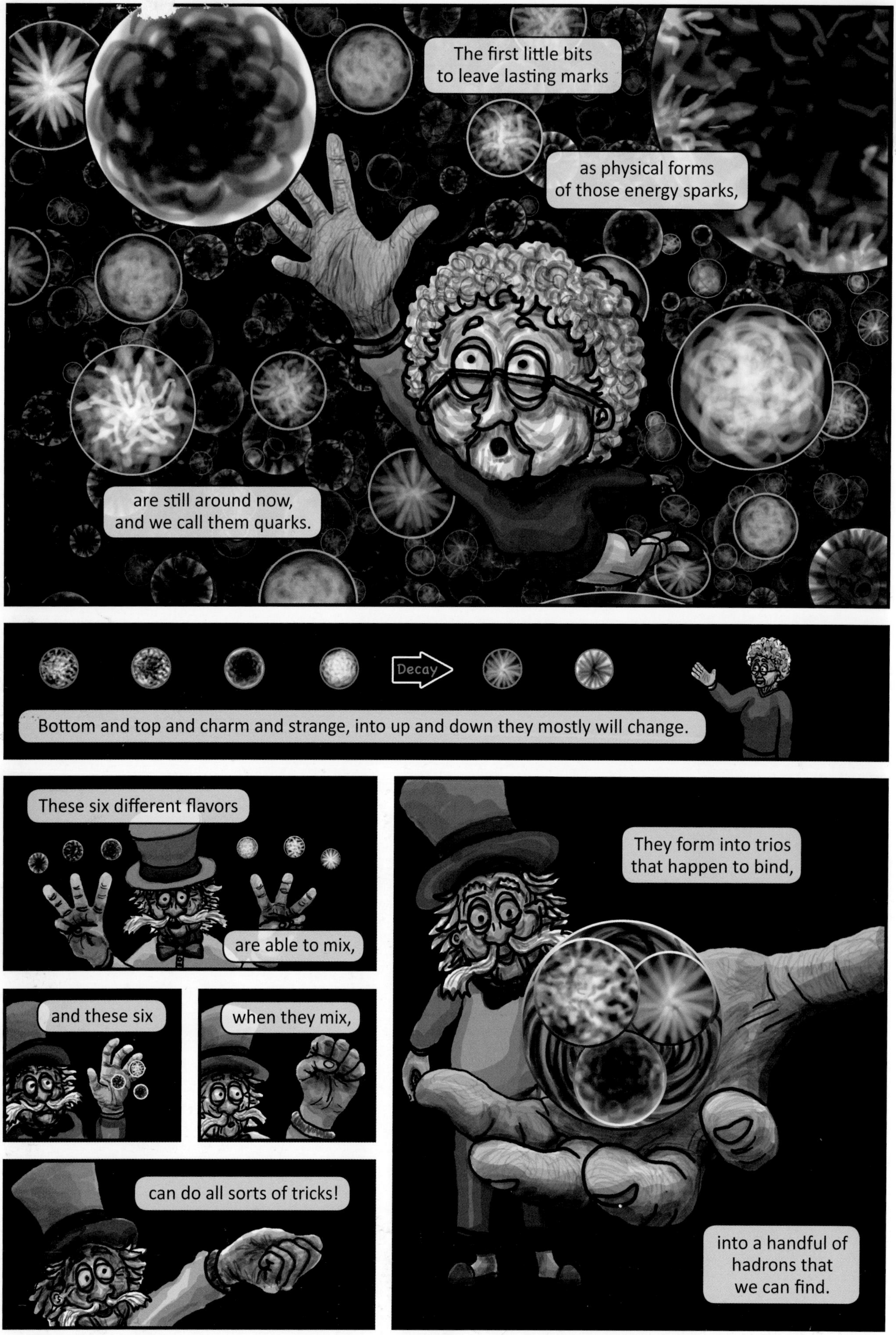

The first little bits
to leave lasting marks
as physical forms
of those energy sparks,
are still around now,
and we call them quarks.
Decay
Bottom and top and charm and strange, into up and down they mostly will change.
These six different flavors
are able to mix,
and these six
when they mix,
can do all sorts of tricks!
They form into trios
that happen to bind,
into a handful of
hadrons that
we can find.

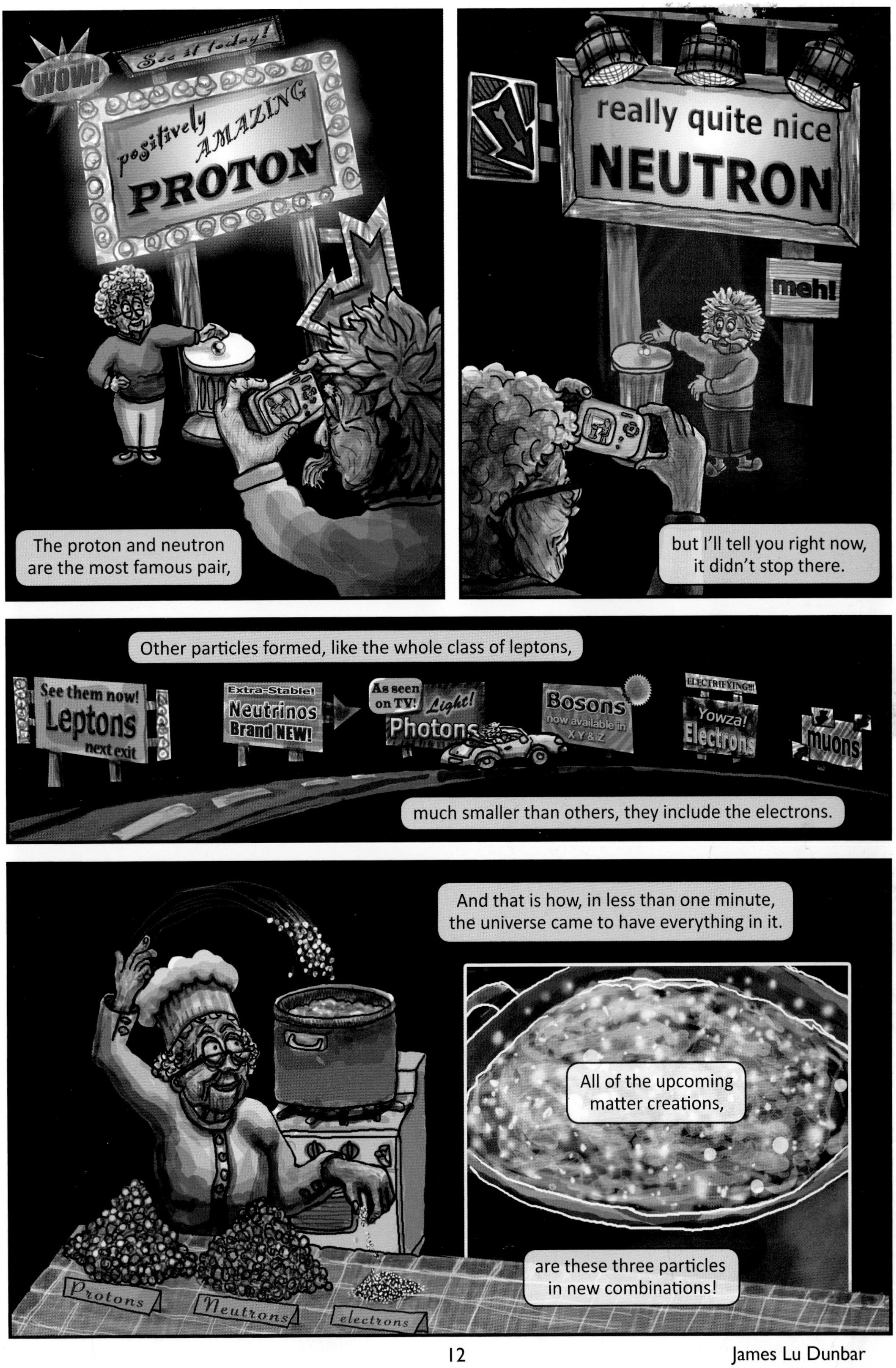
WOW!
See it today!
positively AMAZING PROTON
The proton and neutron
are the most famous pair,
really quite nice NEUTRON
meh!
but I'll tell you right now,
it didn't stop there.
Other particles formed, like the whole class of leptons,
See them now! Leptons next exit
Extra-Stable! Neutrinos Brand NEW!
As seen on TV! Light! Photons
Bosons now available in X Y & Z
ELECTRIFYING!!! Yowza! Electrons
muons
much smaller than others, they include the electrons.
And that is how, in less than one minute,
the universe came to have everything in it.
All of the upcoming
matter creations,
are these three particles
in new combinations!
Protons
Neutrons
electrons

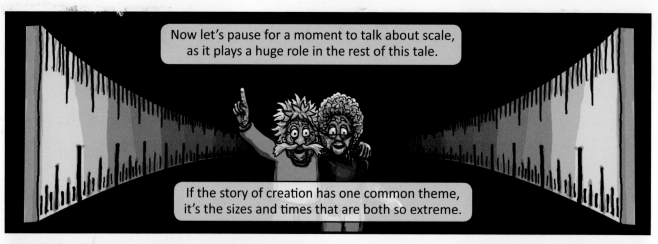

Now let's pause for a moment to talk about scale,
as it plays a huge role in the rest of this tale.

If the story of creation has one common theme,
it's the sizes and times that are both so extreme.

Some things happen so fast, they're hard to believe.

Some things are too small
for our eyes to perceive.

Like the proton and neutron,

so very scant,

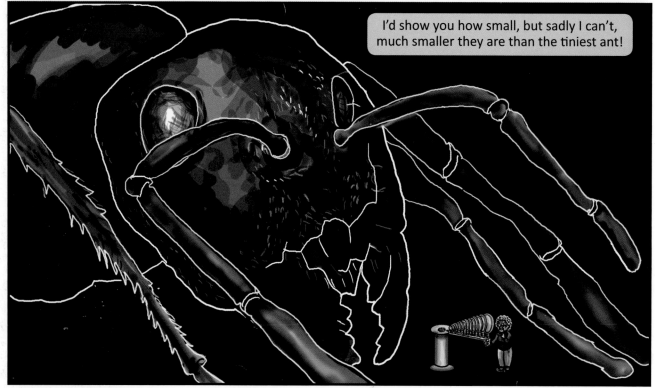

I'd show you how small, but sadly I can't,
much smaller they are than the tiniest ant!

Some things are larger than you thought things could be,

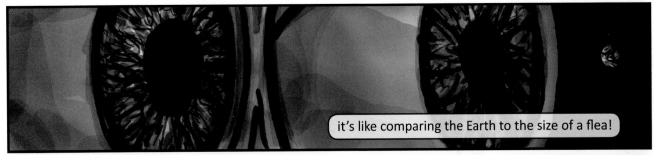

it's like comparing the Earth to the size of a flea!

And some of the change that slowly appears,

takes thousands

of thousands

of thousands

of years!

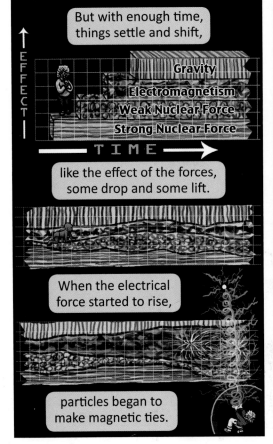

But with enough time, things settle and shift,

EFFECT

Gravity
Electromagnetism
Weak Nuclear Force
Strong Nuclear Force

TIME

like the effect of the forces, some drop and some lift.

When the electrical force started to rise,

particles began to make magnetic ties.

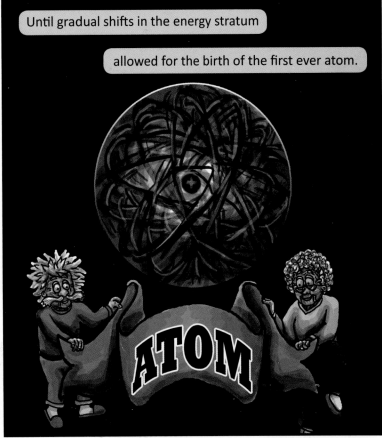

Until gradual shifts in the energy stratum

allowed for the birth of the first ever atom.

ATOM

James Lu Dunbar

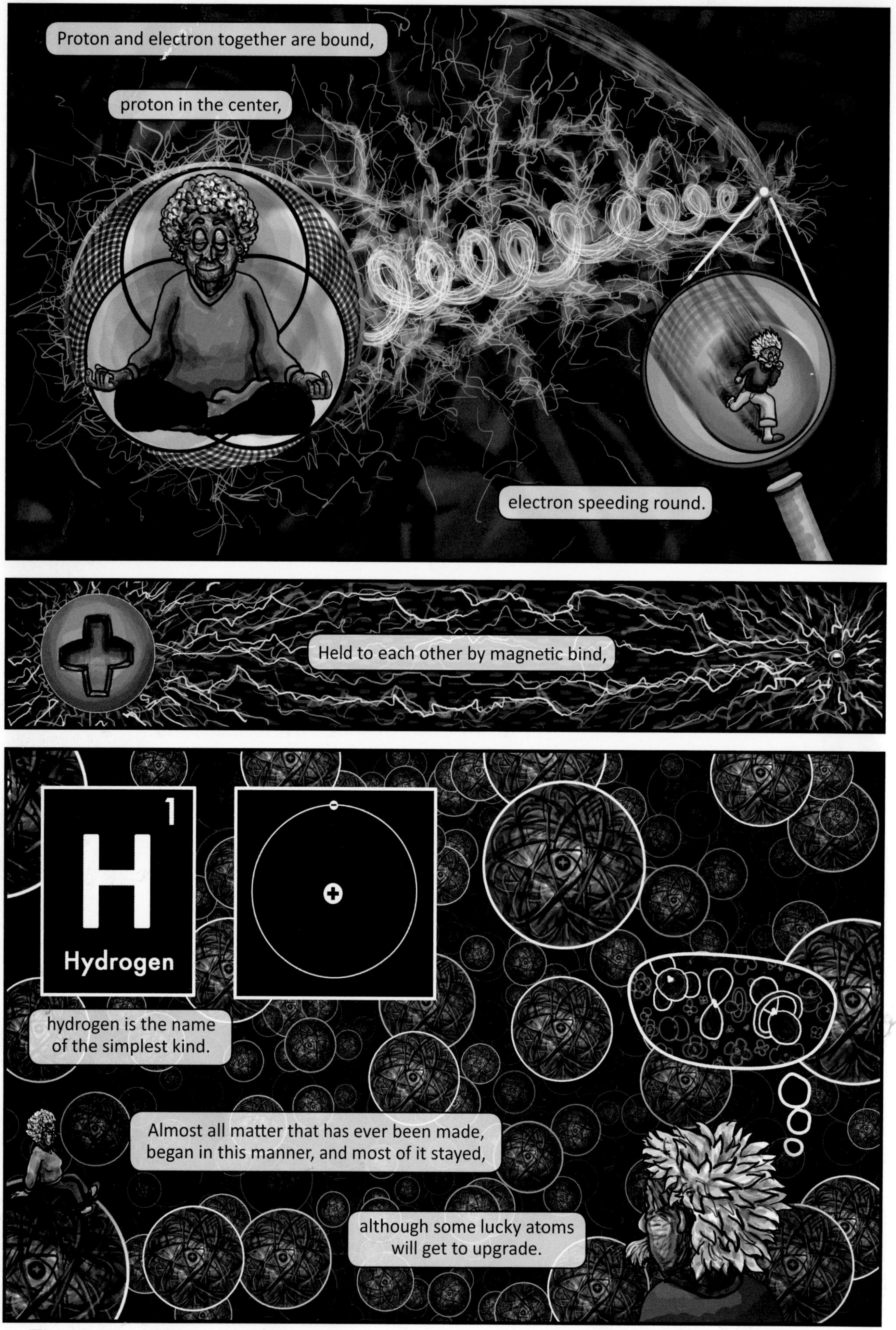
Proton and electron together are bound,
proton in the center,
electron speeding round.
Held to each other by magnetic bind,
H
1
Hydrogen
hydrogen is the name
of the simplest kind.
Almost all matter that has ever been made,
began in this manner, and most of it stayed,
although some lucky atoms
will get to upgrade.

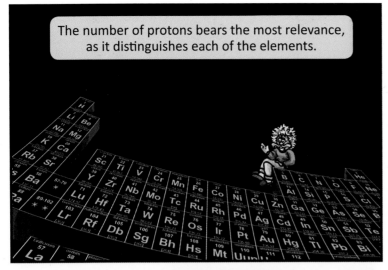

The number of protons bears the most relevance, as it distinguishes each of the elements.

Although I suppose it worthwhile to mention, for the sake of a fuller, more sound comprehension,

the proton in the center may not be alone, as another has access to this VIP zone.

The neutron may not be quite as attractive, but it's quiet, well-mannered, and rarely reactive.

And because of that fact we now shall return, to the protons, which are of greater concern.

Hydrogen has one,

and helium two,

lithium three,

and for the moment we're through,

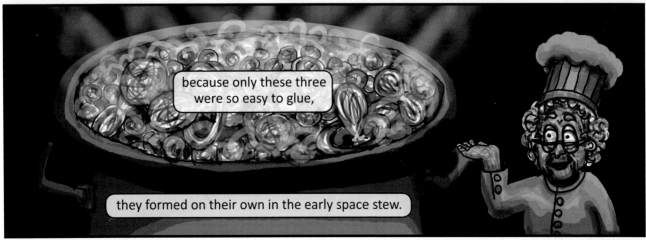

because only these three were so easy to glue,

they formed on their own in the early space stew.

16

James Lu Dunbar

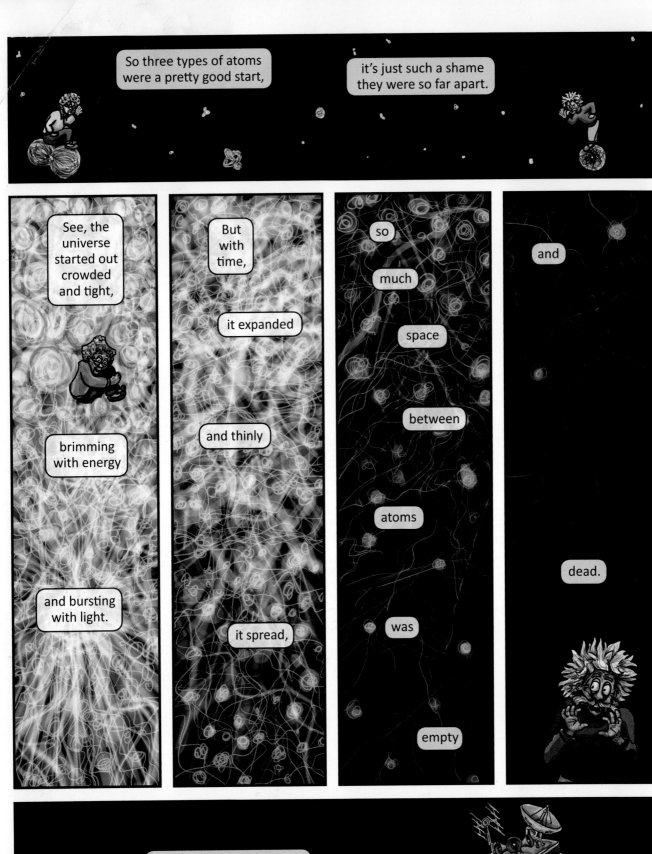

So three types of atoms were a pretty good start,

it's just such a shame they were so far apart.

See, the universe started out crowded and tight,

brimming with energy

and bursting with light.

But with time,

it expanded

and thinly

it spread,

so

much

space

between

atoms

was

empty

and

dead.

Lonely and cold and dark as midnight, *What could have saved us from such a plight?*

Gravity gives matter a small constant pull, great for a universe that isn't so full.

It means every atom, through all of existence,

is pulled to the others by gravity's insistence.

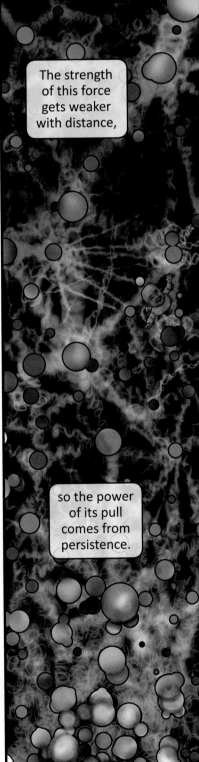

The strength of this force gets weaker with distance,

so the power of its pull comes from persistence.

Over time, it would act as a great cosmic girdle,

as the thinly spread matter

would eventually curdle.

James Lu Dunbar

Gas would amass into great cloudy lumps,

a fast-spinning class of protostellar clumps.

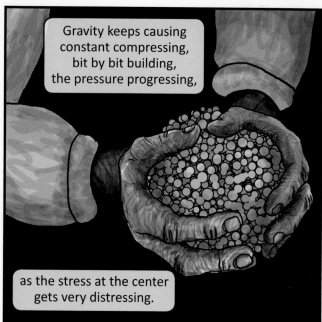

Gravity keeps causing constant compressing, bit by bit building, the pressure progressing,

as the stress at the center gets very distressing.

So much that our clump becomes such a tight ball,

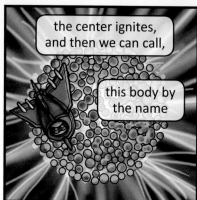

the center ignites, and then we can call,

this body by the name

that is brightest of all.

This thing that allows us to be who we are, the explosion inside has made it a star!

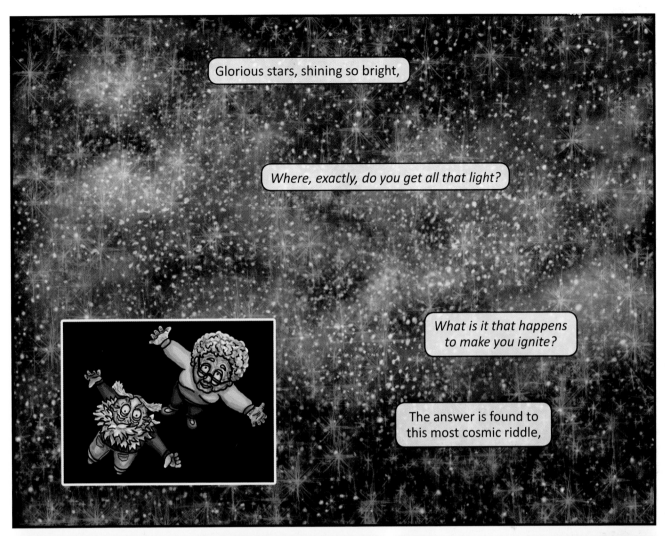

Glorious stars, shining so bright,

Where, exactly, do you get all that light?

What is it that happens to make you ignite?

The answer is found to this most cosmic riddle,

deep down inside of the star's very middle,

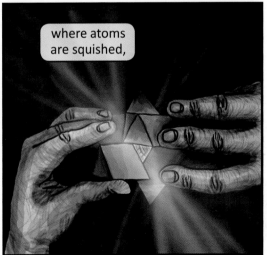

where atoms are squished,

so much

that they fiddle.

James Lu Dunbar

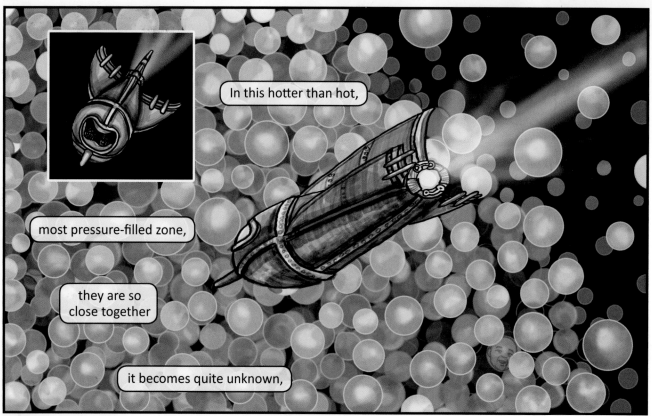

In this hotter than hot,

most pressure-filled zone,

they are so close together

it becomes quite unknown,

to the atoms just exactly which electrons they own.

And if it wasn't enough,

not knowing who's whose,

WARNING POSSIBLE FUSION

they get pushed

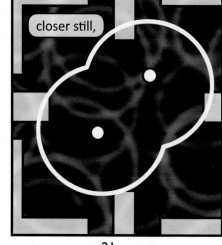

closer still,

till whole atoms fuse.

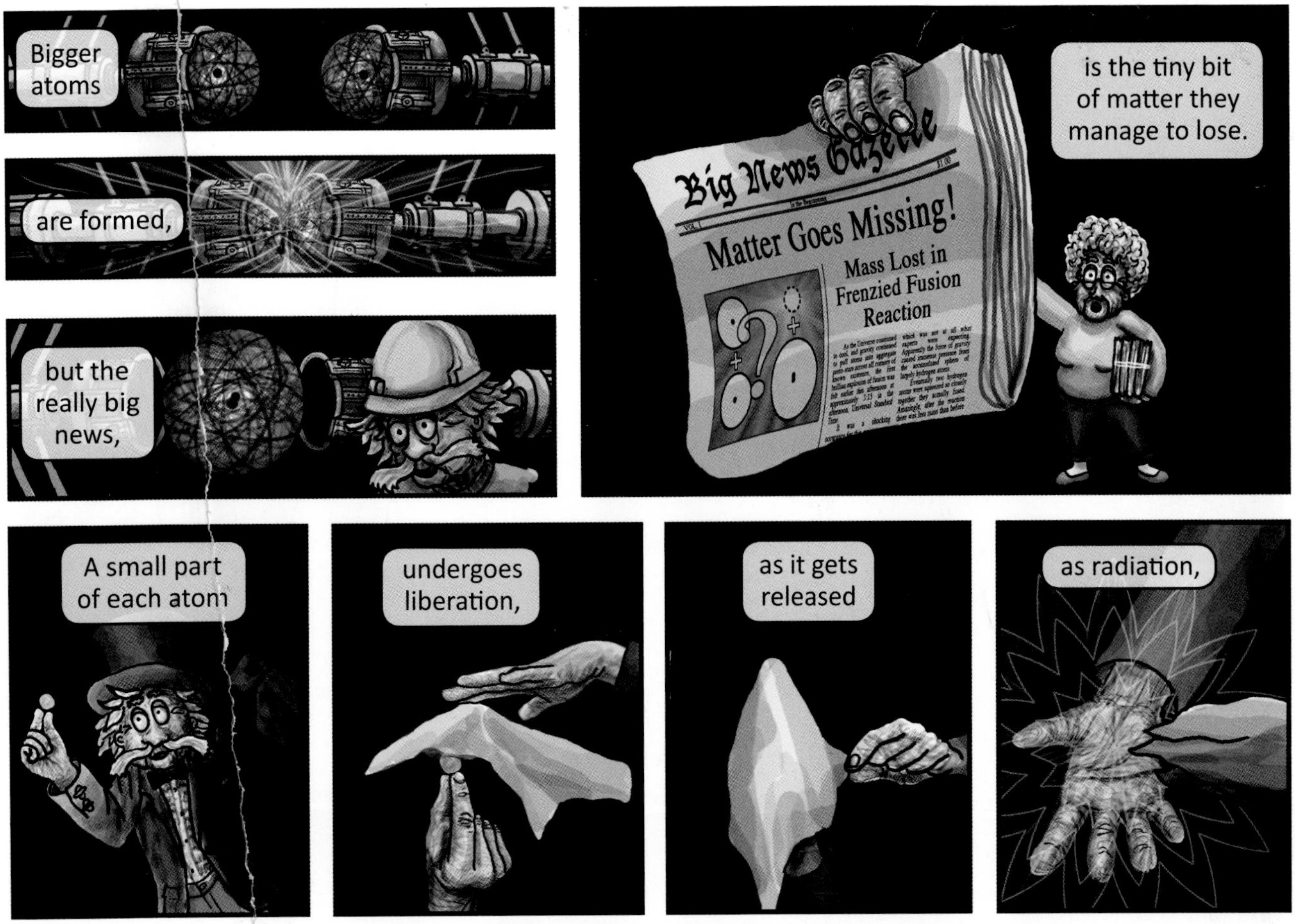
Bigger atoms
are formed,
but the really big news,
is the tiny bit of matter they manage to lose.
Big News Gazette
Matter Goes Missing!
Mass Lost in Frenzied Fusion Reaction
A small part of each atom
undergoes liberation,
as it gets released
as radiation,

in accordance with that most famous equation,
whose marvelous meaning can now be shared, assuming, of course, that you are prepared,

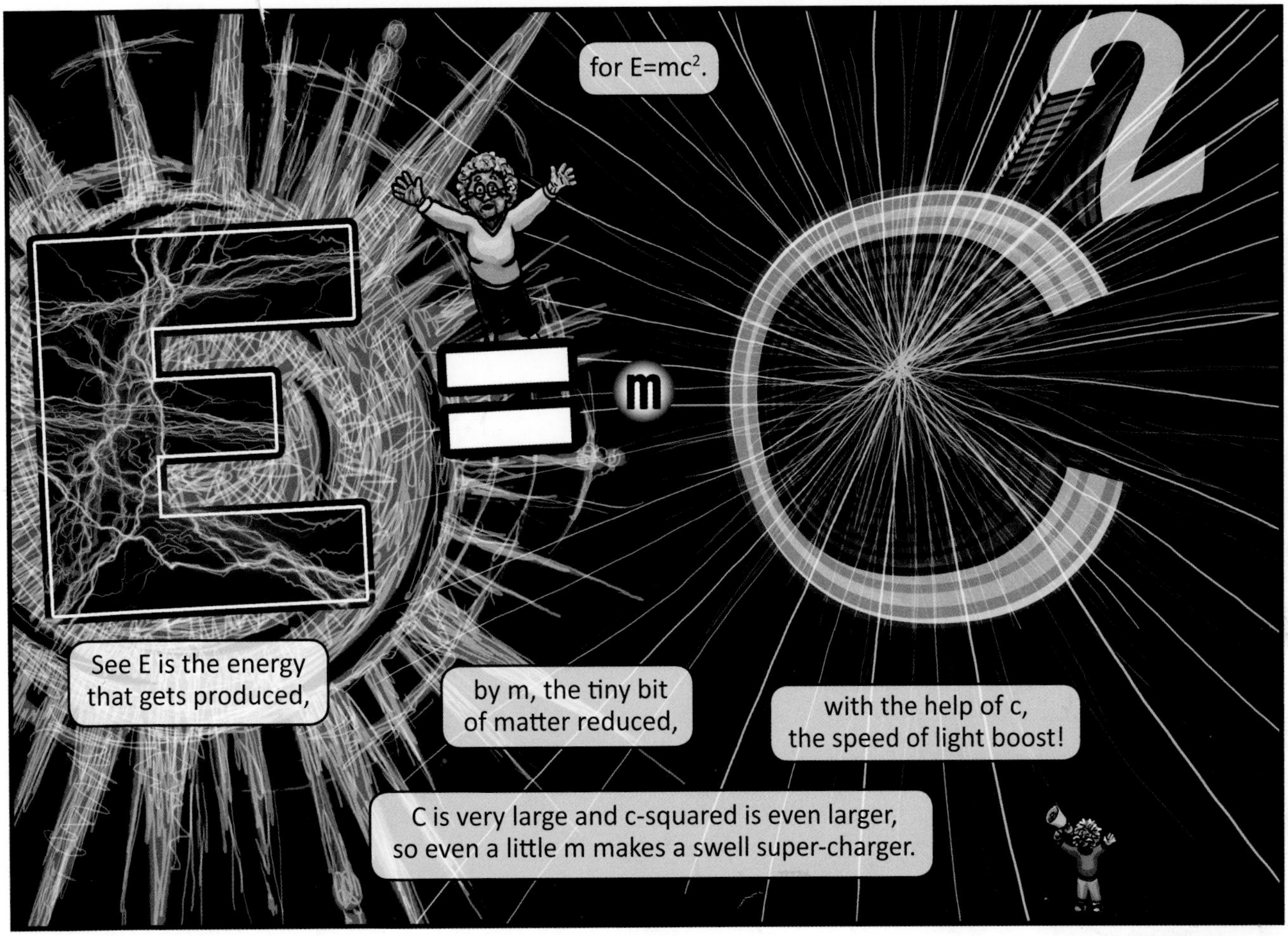
for E=mc².
E = m c 2
See E is the energy that gets produced,
by m, the tiny bit of matter reduced,
with the help of c, the speed of light boost!
C is very large and c-squared is even larger, so even a little m makes a swell super-charger.

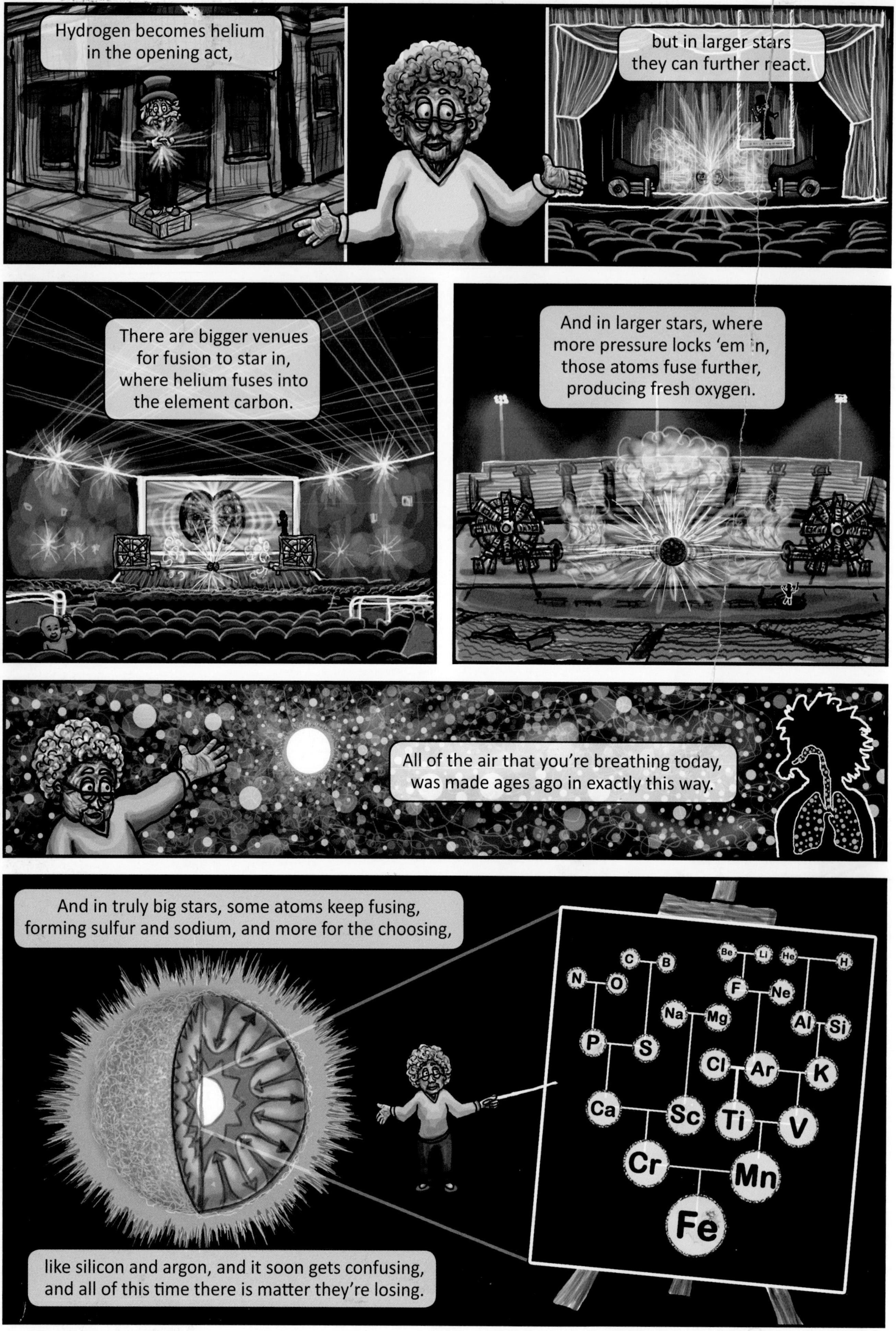
Hydrogen becomes helium in the opening act,
but in larger stars they can further react.
There are bigger venues for fusion to star in, where helium fuses into the element carbon.
And in larger stars, where more pressure locks 'em in, those atoms fuse further, producing fresh oxygen.
All of the air that you're breathing today, was made ages ago in exactly this way.
And in truly big stars, some atoms keep fusing, forming sulfur and sodium, and more for the choosing,
N O C B Be Li He H F Ne Na Mg Al Si P S Cl Ar K Ca Sc Ti V Cr Mn Fe
like silicon and argon, and it soon gets confusing, and all of this time there is matter they're losing.

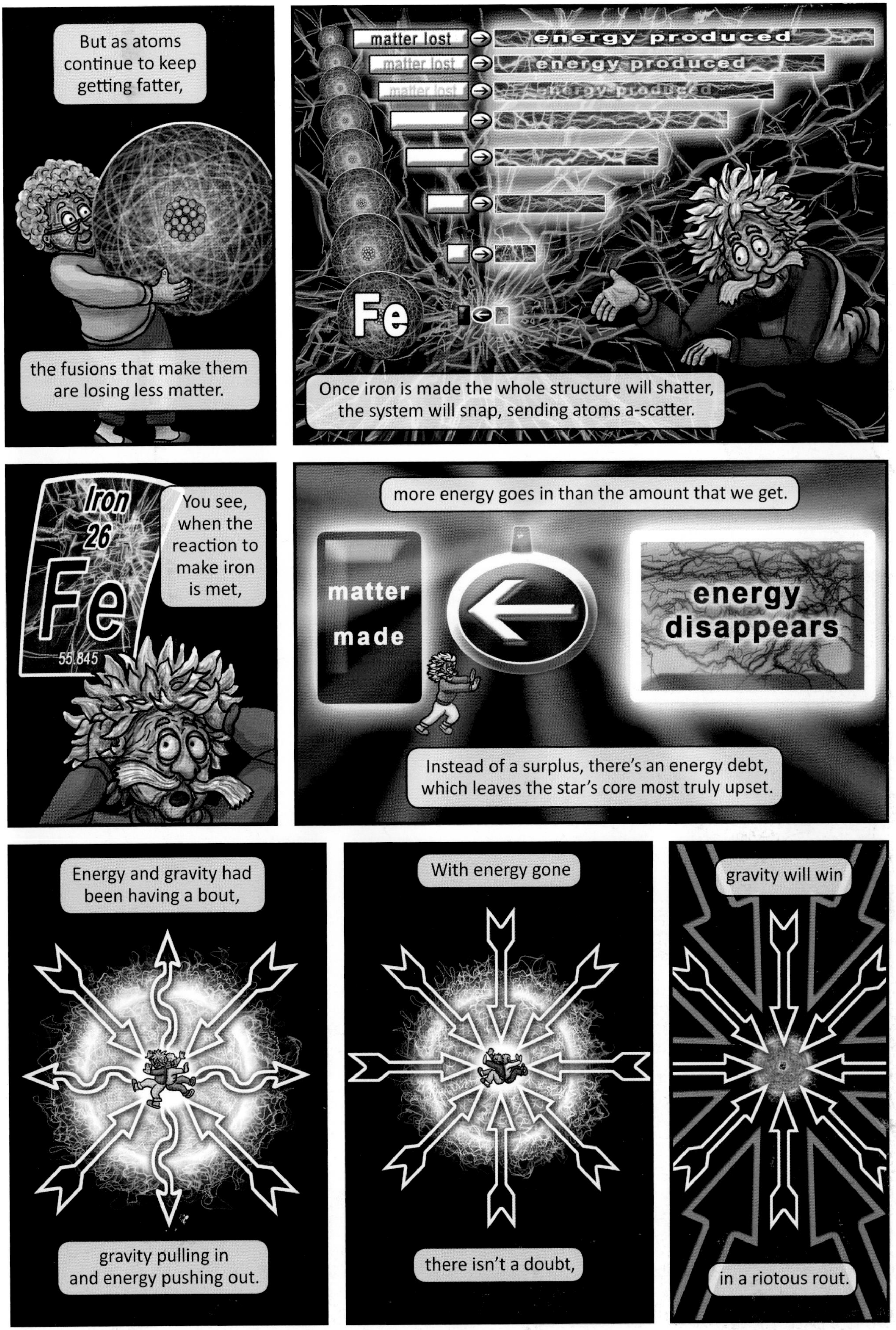
But as atoms continue to keep getting fatter,
the fusions that make them are losing less matter.
matter lost
energy produced
matter lost
energy produced
matter lost
energy produced
Fe
Once iron is made the whole structure will shatter, the system will snap, sending atoms a-scatter.
Iron
26
Fe
55.845
You see, when the reaction to make iron is met,
more energy goes in than the amount that we get.
matter made
energy disappears
Instead of a surplus, there's an energy debt, which leaves the star's core most truly upset.
Energy and gravity had been having a bout,
gravity pulling in and energy pushing out.
With energy gone
there isn't a doubt,
gravity will win
in a riotous rout.

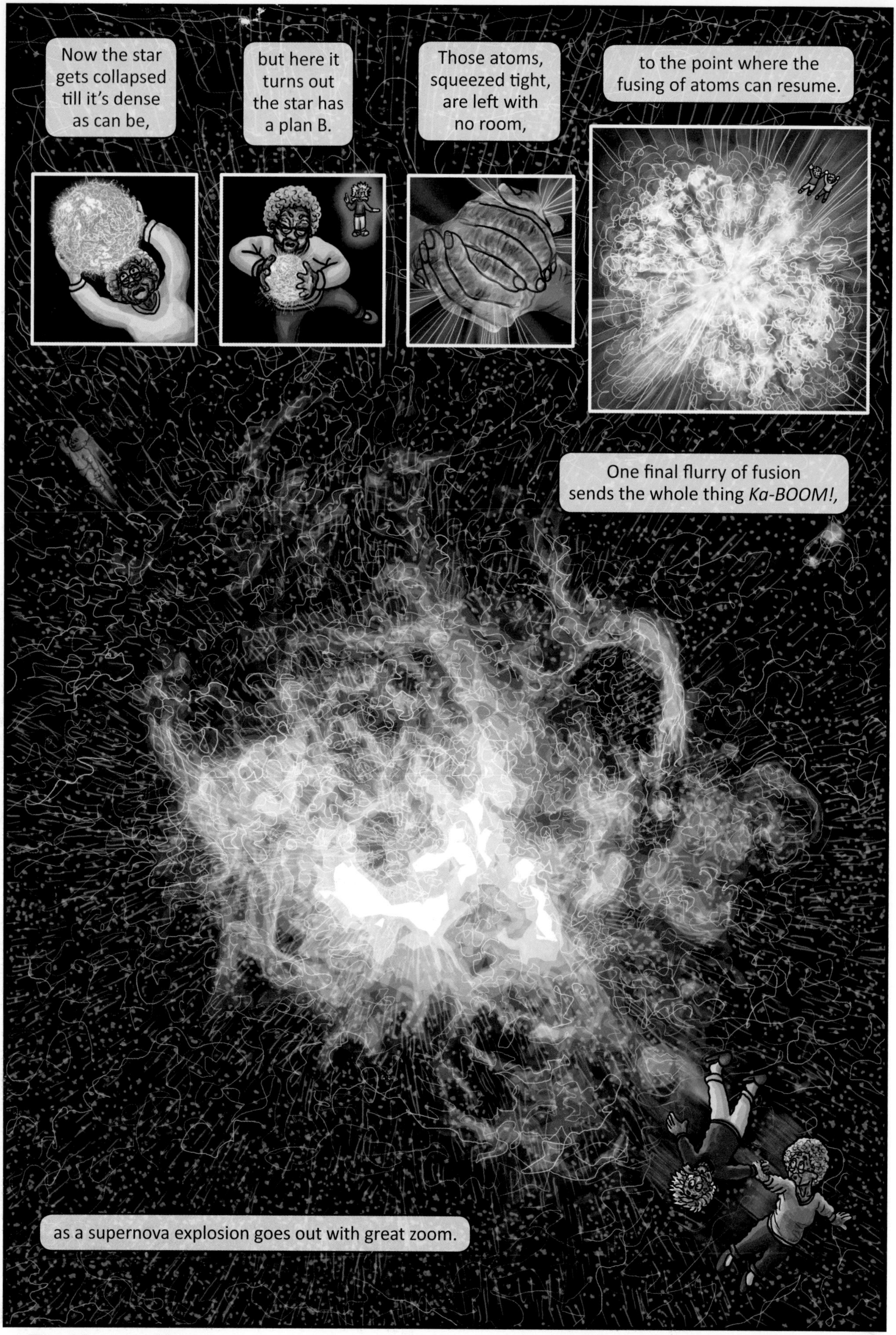
Now the star gets collapsed till it's dense as can be,
but here it turns out the star has a plan B.
Those atoms, squeezed tight, are left with no room,
to the point where the fusing of atoms can resume.
One final flurry of fusion sends the whole thing *Ka-BOOM!*,
as a supernova explosion goes out with great zoom.

It's the only thing known to make heavier elements,

plus spread them around with such explosive elegance.

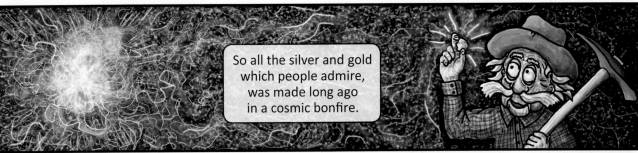

So all the silver and gold which people admire, was made long ago in a cosmic bonfire.

These stars were destroyed,

but don't be forlorn,

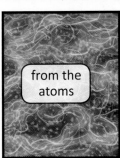

from the atoms

they spread,

new stars could be born,

and one of two ghosts might stay there to mourn:

a neutron star, that's smallish but bright,

or a black hole, which sucks in all light.

Both are real dense, with great gravity might, within a star system, they can help hold it tight.

James Lu Dunbar

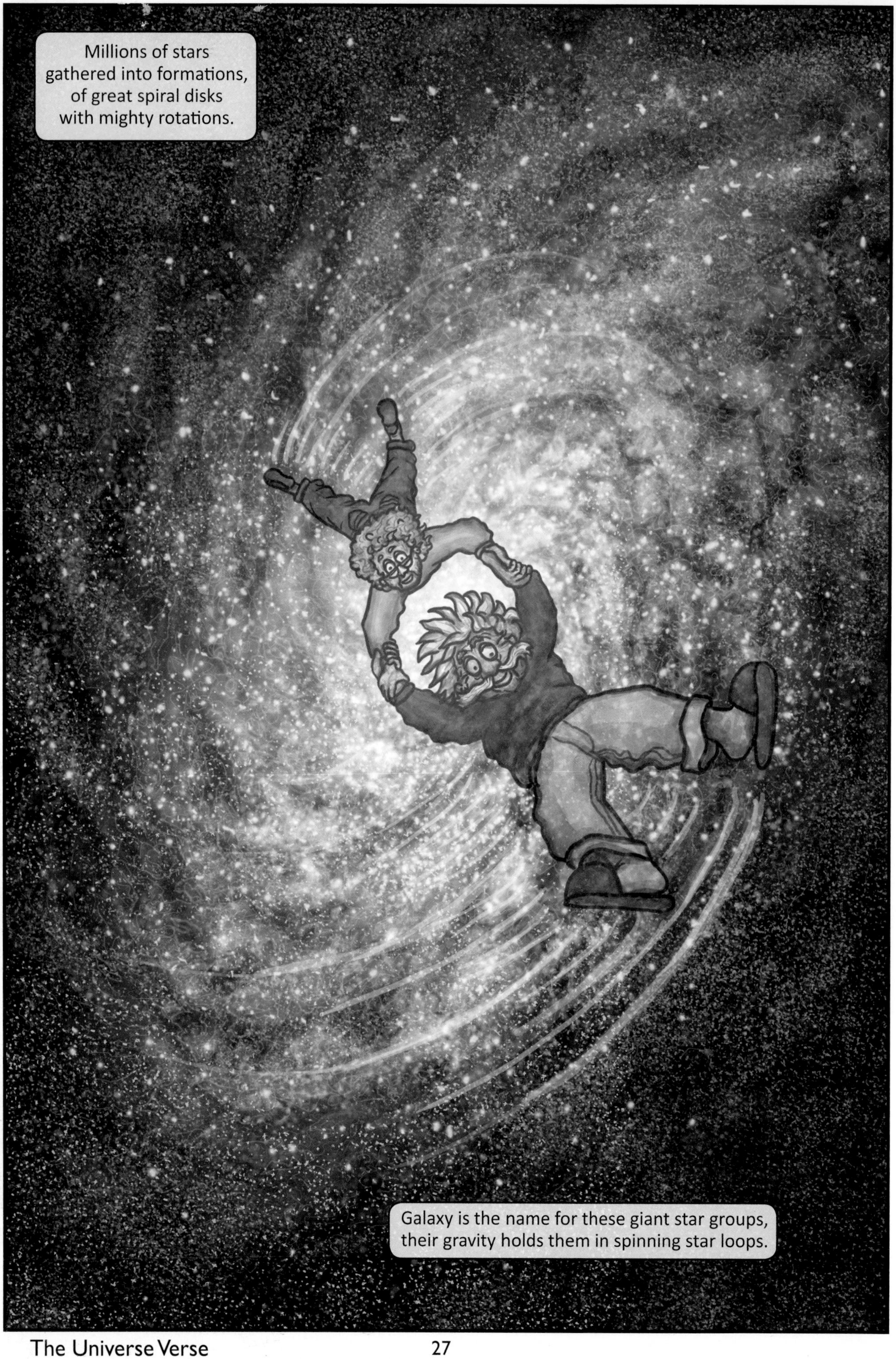
Millions of stars
gathered into formations,
of great spiral disks
with mighty rotations.
Galaxy is the name for these giant star groups,
their gravity holds them in spinning star loops.

The number of galaxies is way past the millions,
made up of stars that number in billions,
and whose atoms add up to some bazillion gajillions!

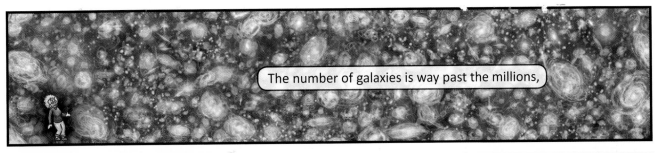

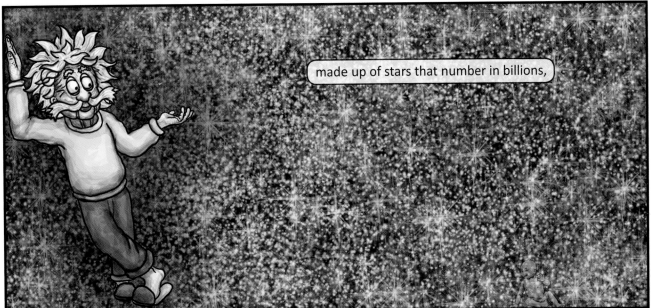

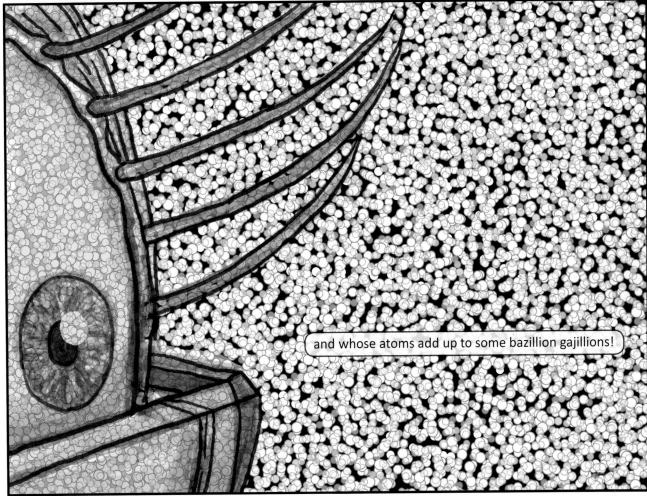

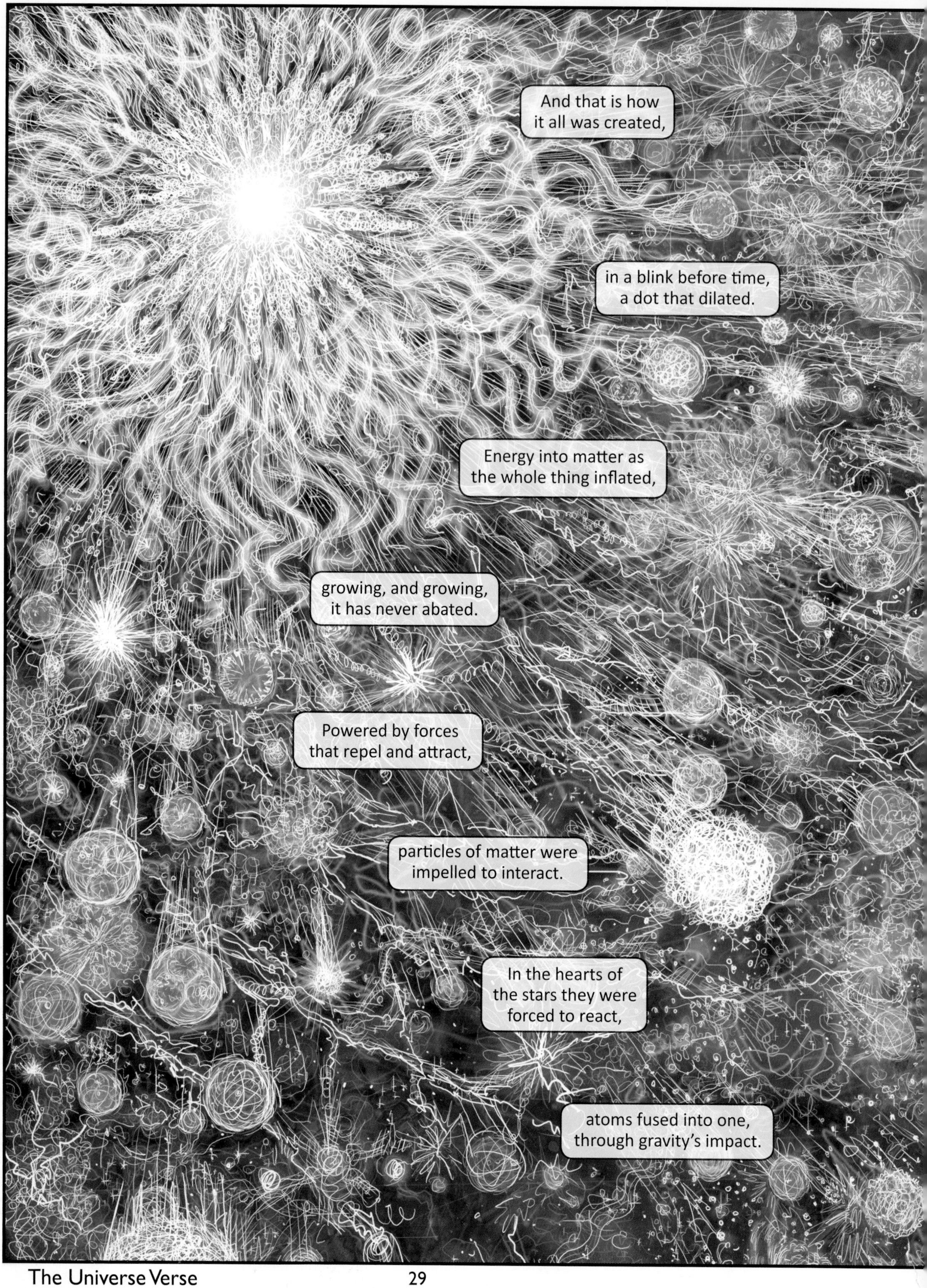
And that is how
it all was created,
in a blink before time,
a dot that dilated.
Energy into matter as
the whole thing inflated,
growing, and growing,
it has never abated.
Powered by forces
that repel and attract,
particles of matter were
impelled to interact.
In the hearts of
the stars they were
forced to react,
atoms fused into one,
through gravity's impact.

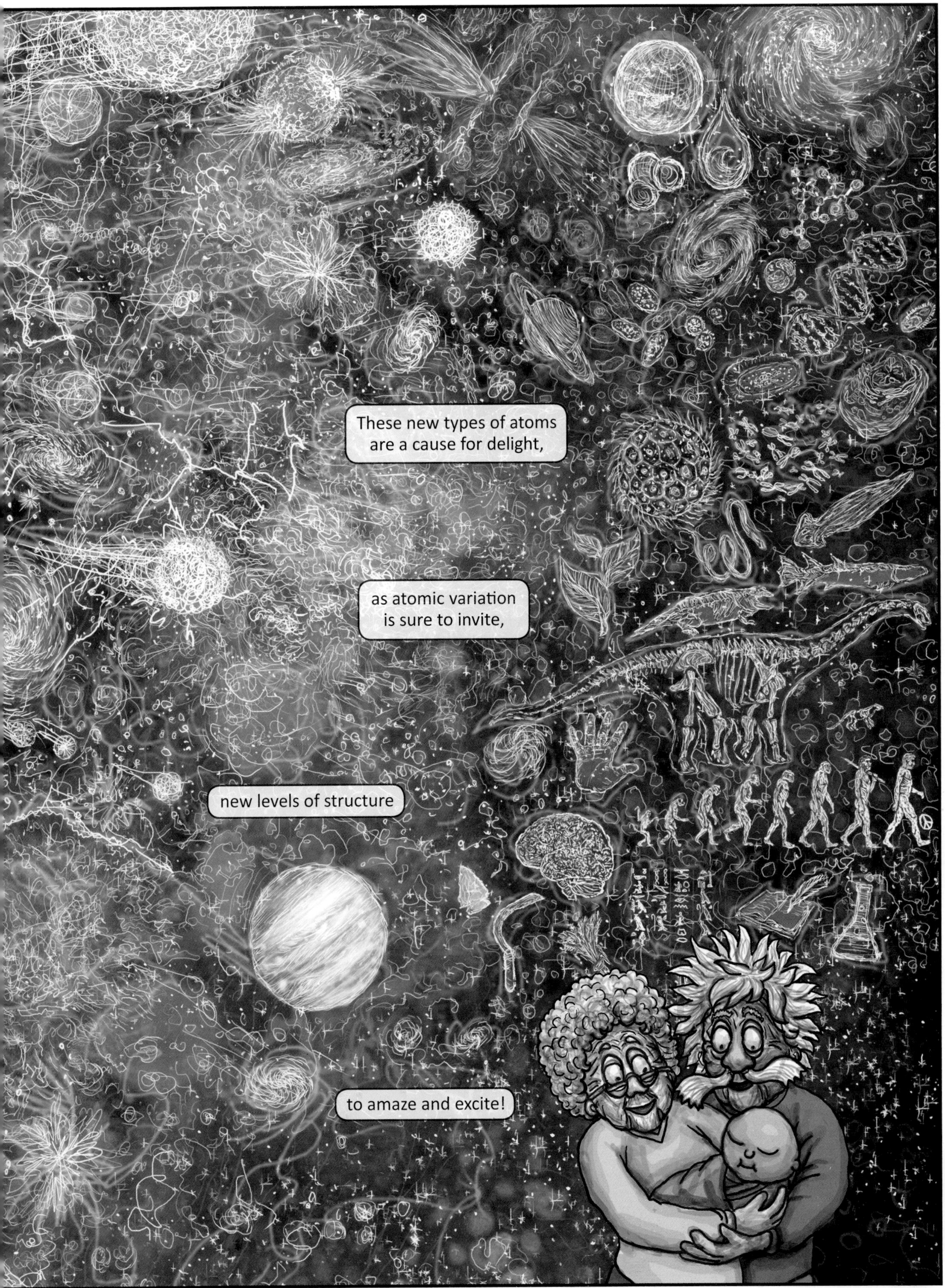
These new types of atoms are a cause for delight,
as atomic variation is sure to invite,
new levels of structure
to amaze and excite!

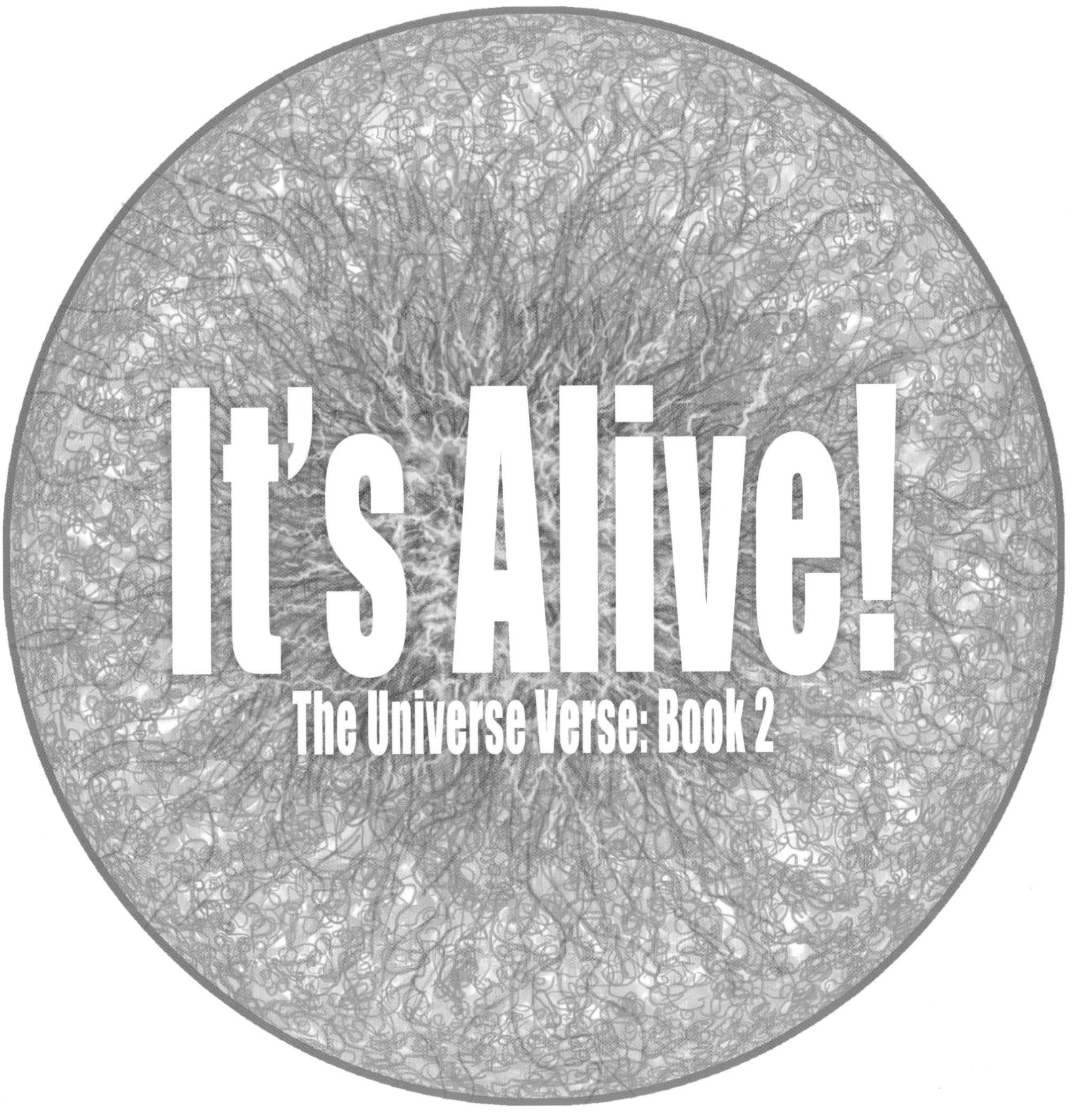
It's Alive!
The Universe Verse: Book 2

There is no wealth but life.

- John Ruskin

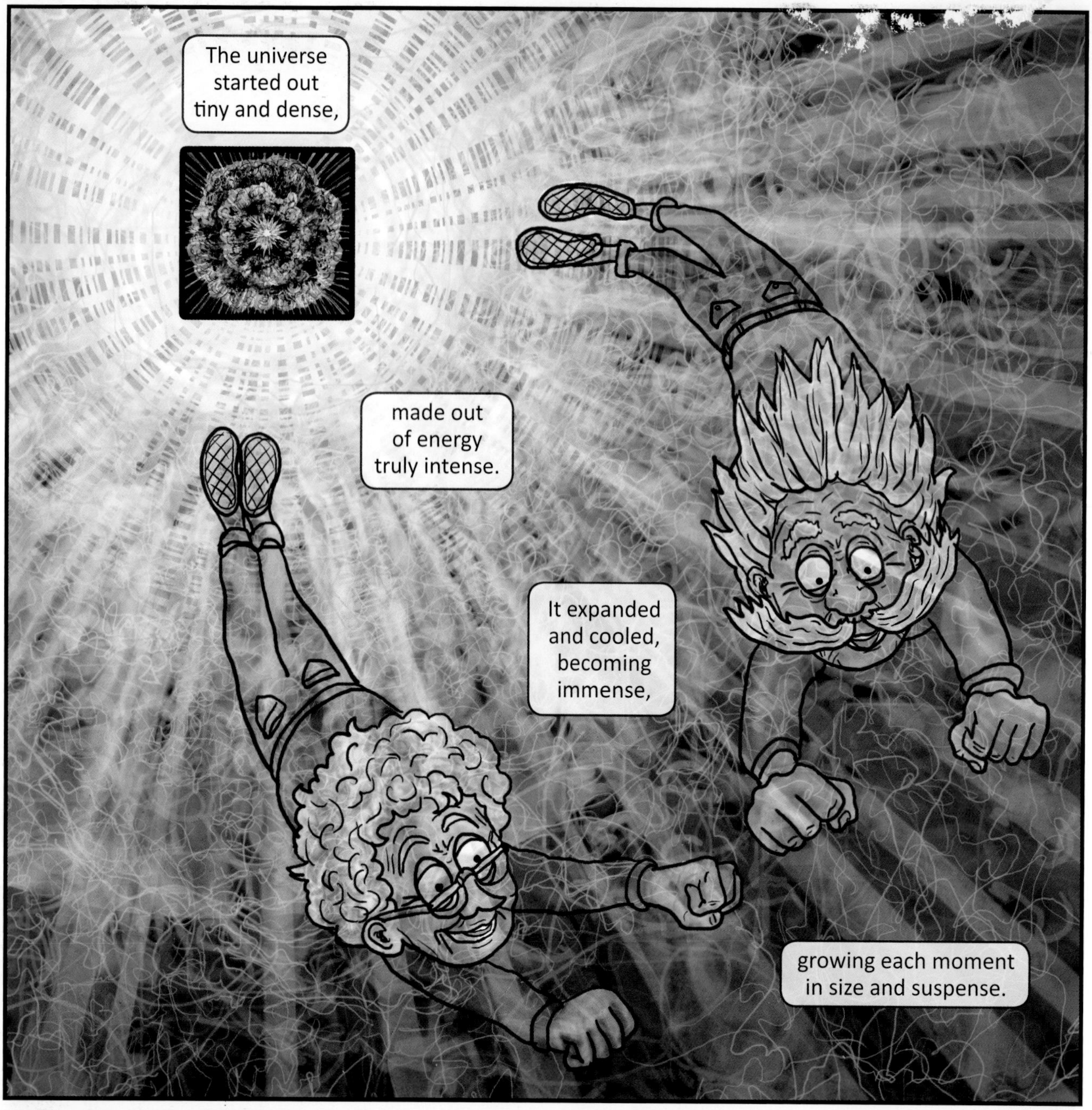
The universe started out tiny and dense,
made out of energy truly intense.
It expanded and cooled, becoming immense,
growing each moment in size and suspense.

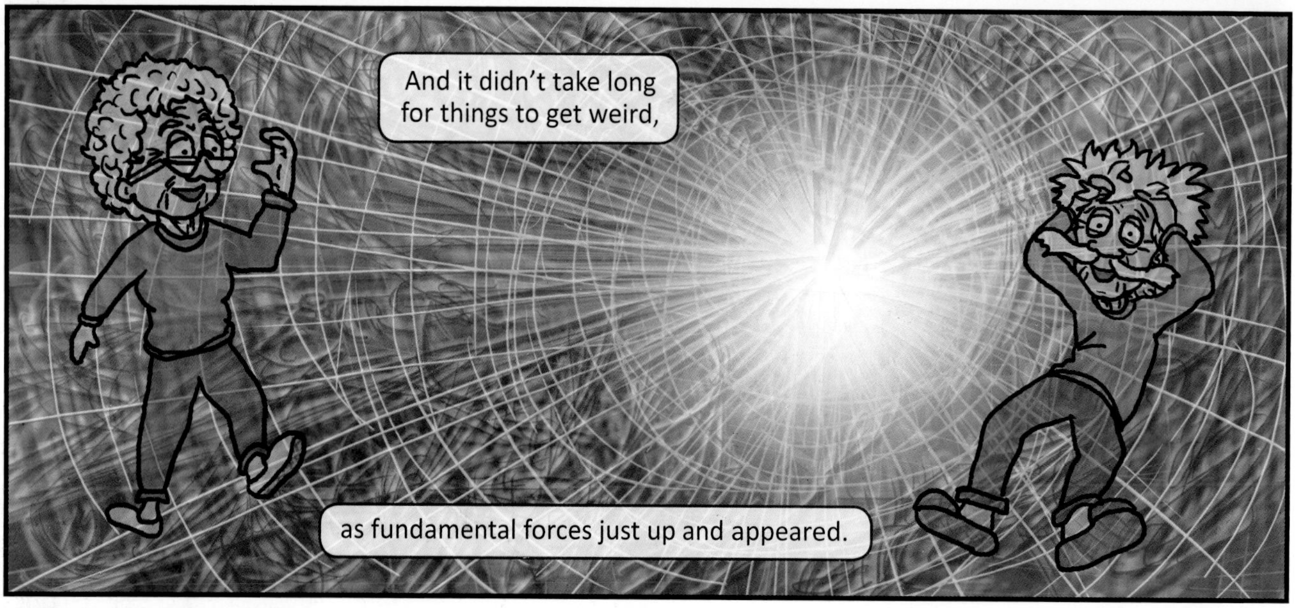
And it didn't take long for things to get weird,
as fundamental forces just up and appeared.

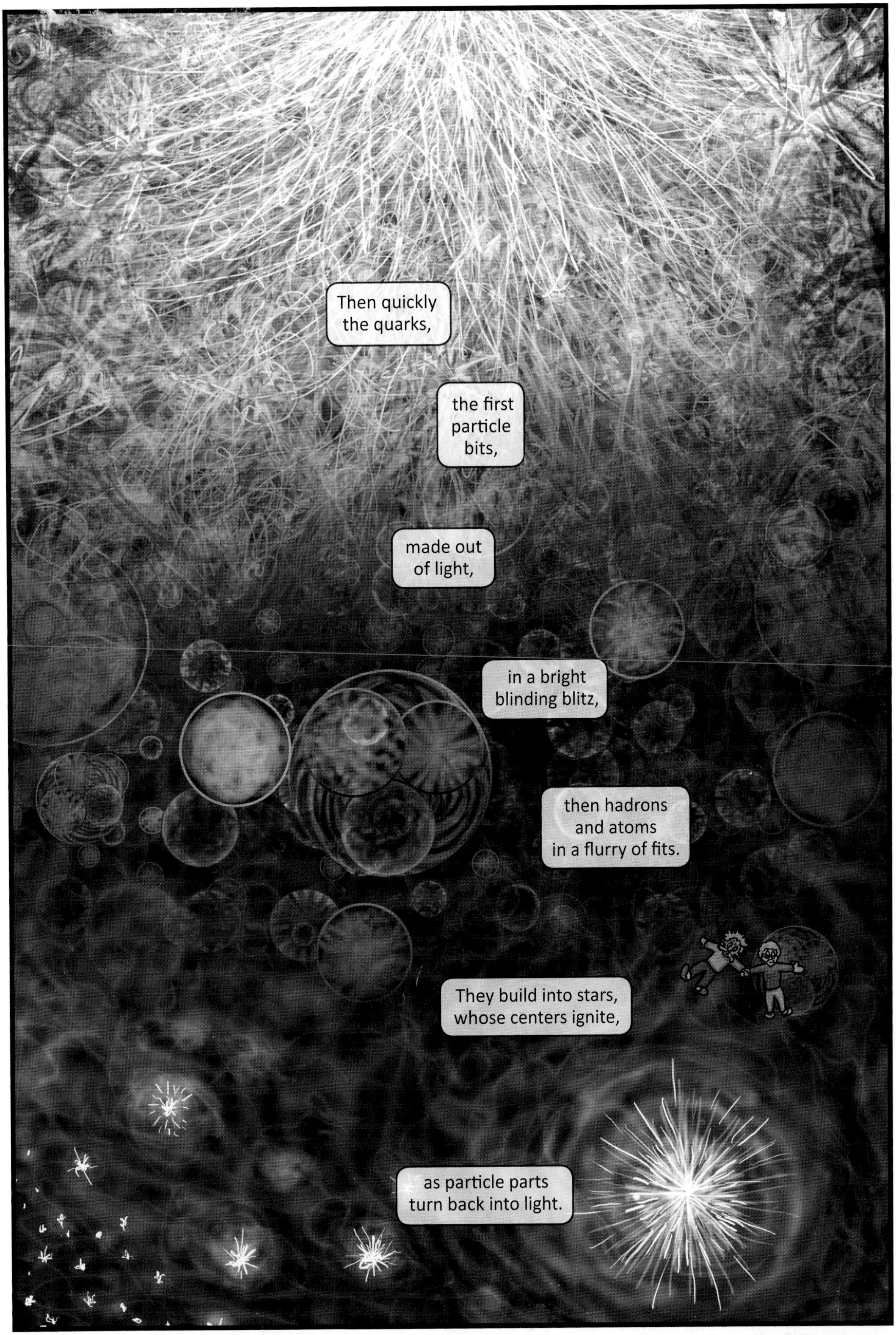
Then quickly the quarks,
the first particle bits,
made out of light,
in a bright blinding blitz,
then hadrons and atoms in a flurry of fits.
They build into stars, whose centers ignite,
as particle parts turn back into light.

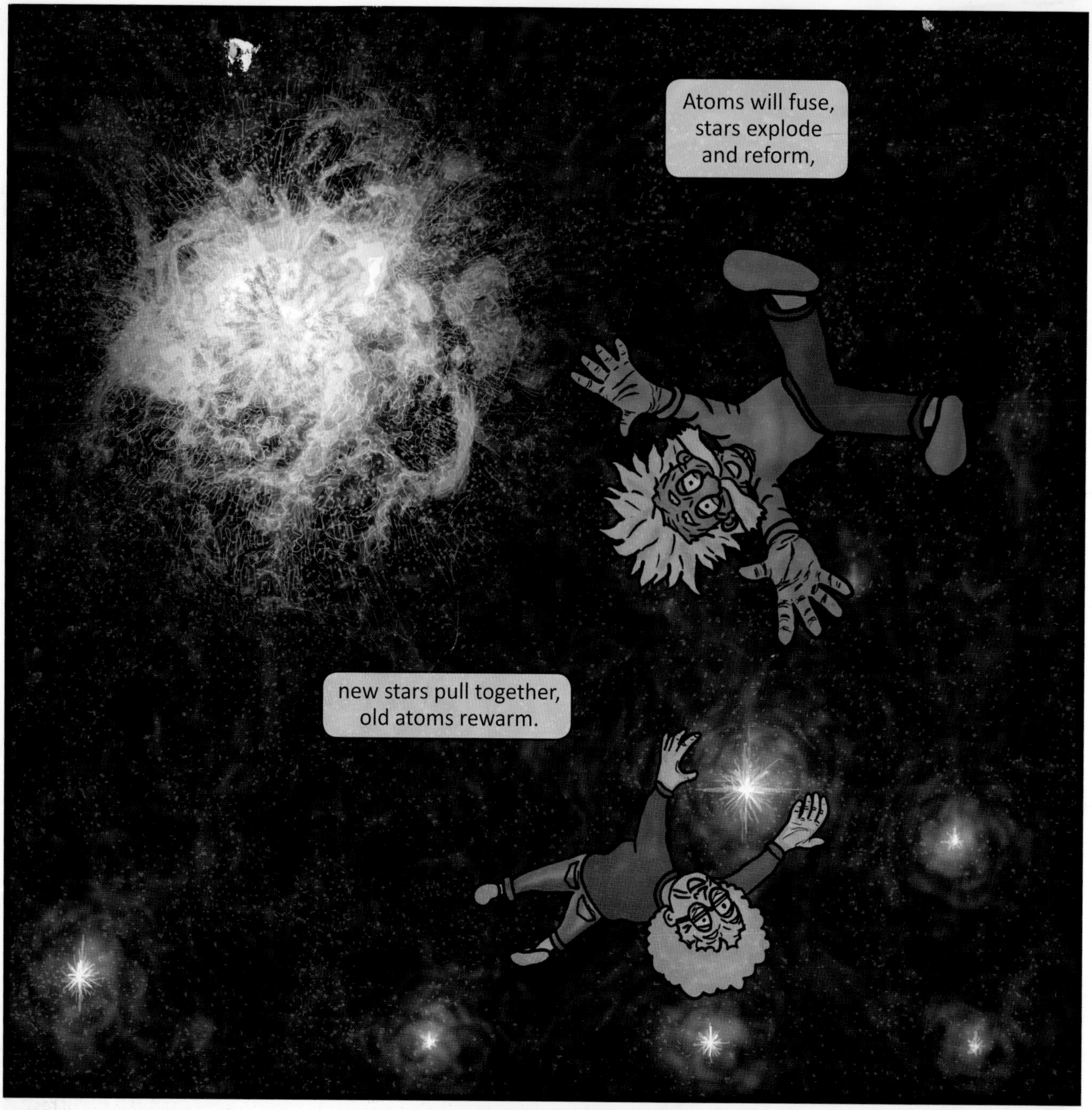
Atoms will fuse,
stars explode
and reform,
new stars pull together,
old atoms rewarm.

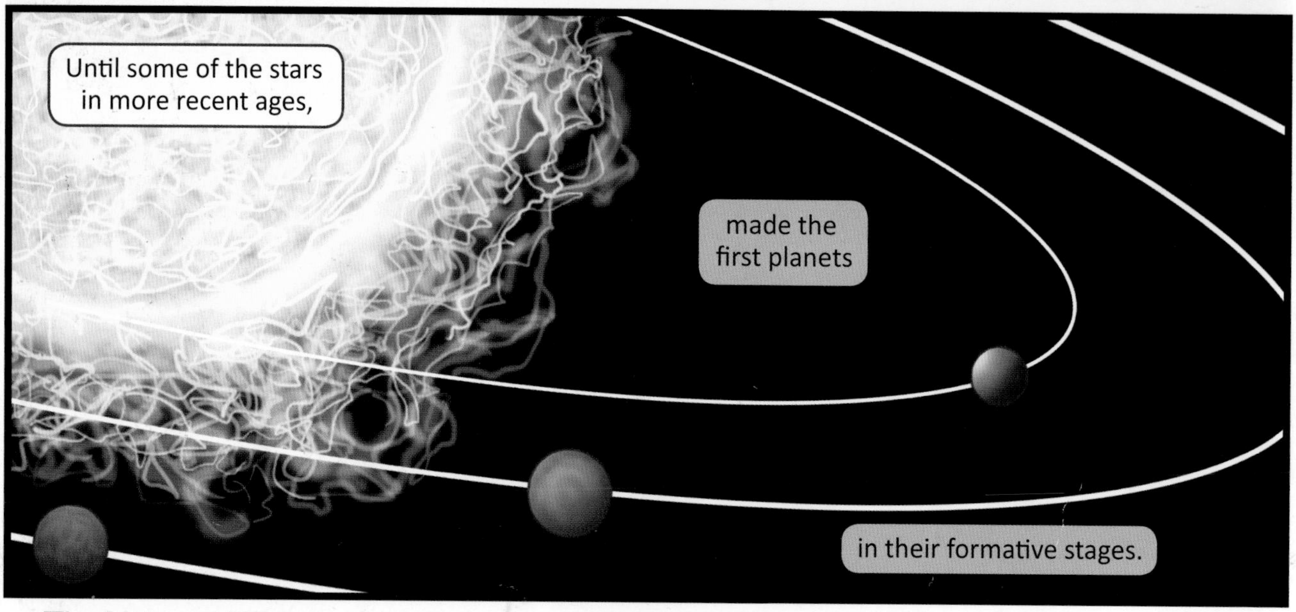
Until some of the stars
in more recent ages,
made the
first planets
in their formative stages.

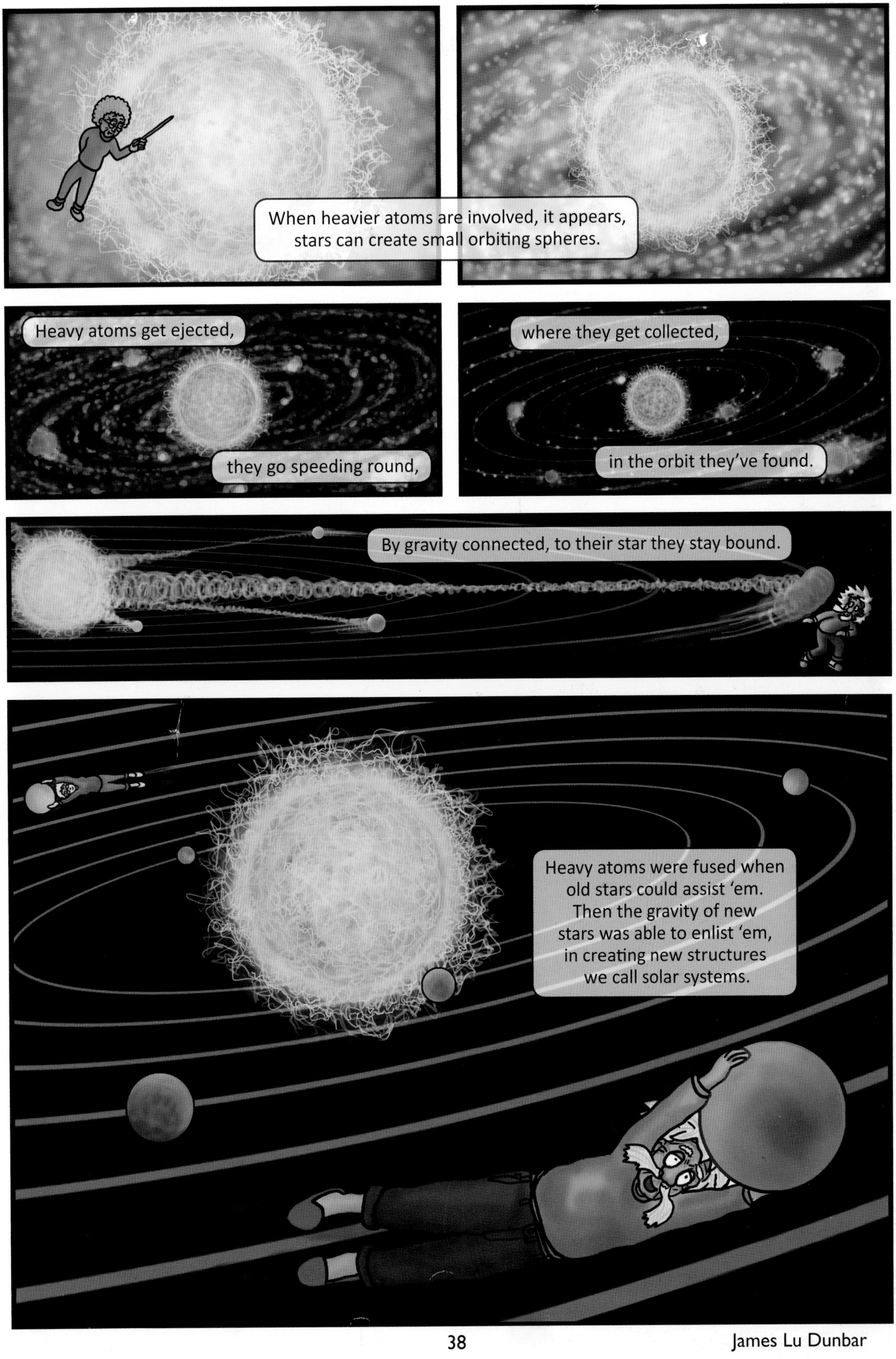
When heavier atoms are involved, it appears,
stars can create small orbiting spheres.
Heavy atoms get ejected,
they go speeding round,
where they get collected,
in the orbit they've found.
By gravity connected, to their star they stay bound.
Heavy atoms were fused when old stars could assist 'em. Then the gravity of new stars was able to enlist 'em, in creating new structures we call solar systems.

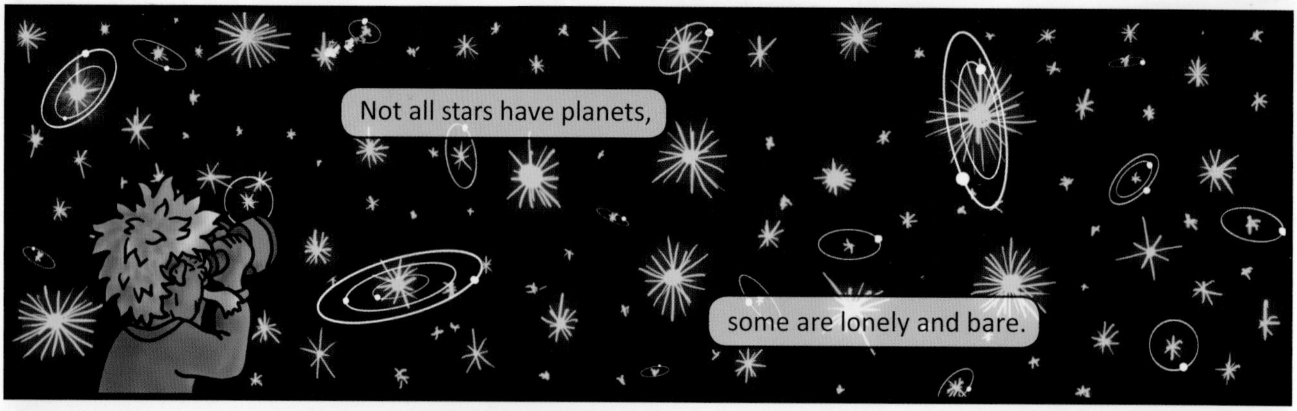
Not all stars have planets,
some are lonely and bare.

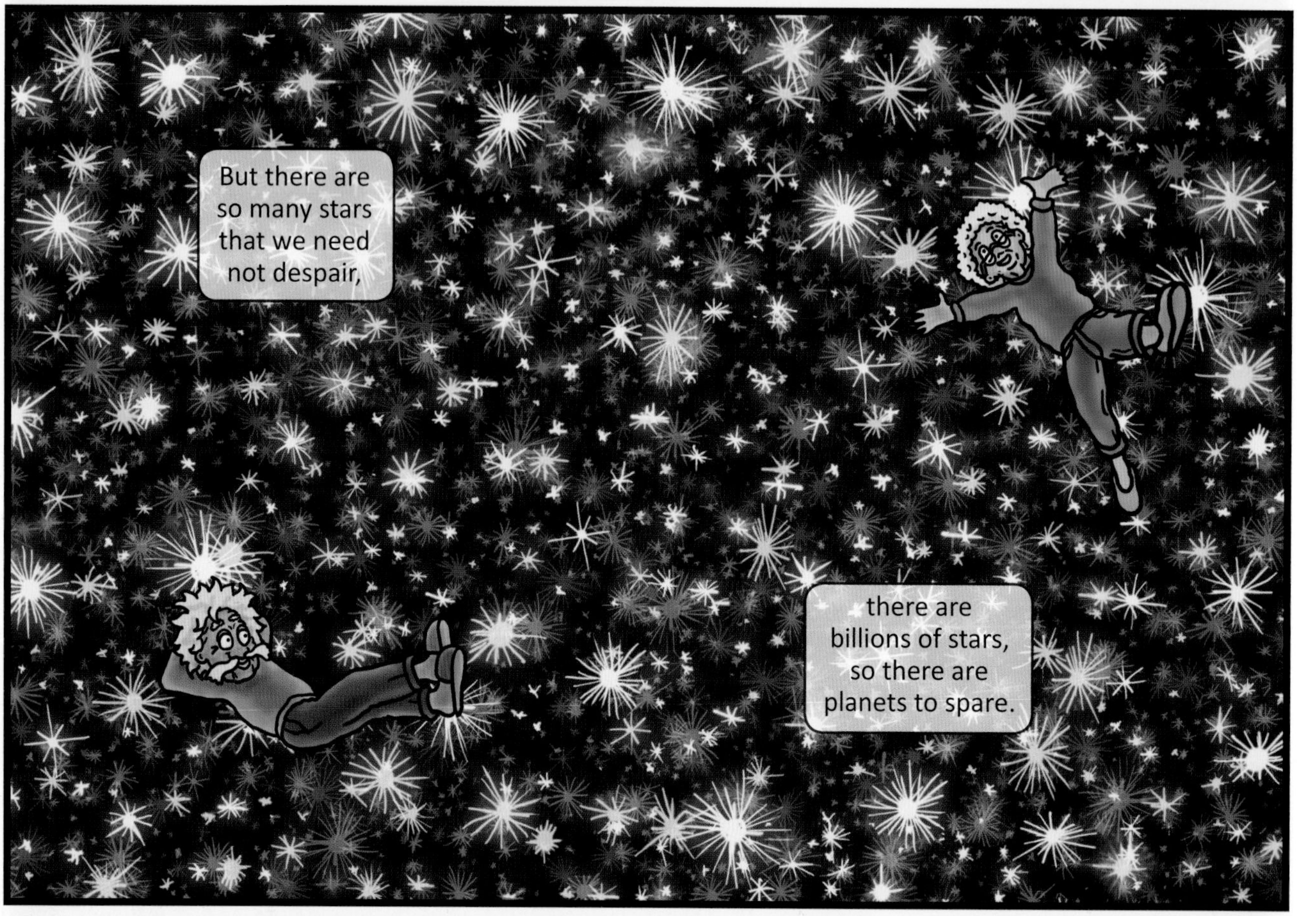
But there are so many stars that we need not despair,
there are billions of stars, so there are planets to spare.

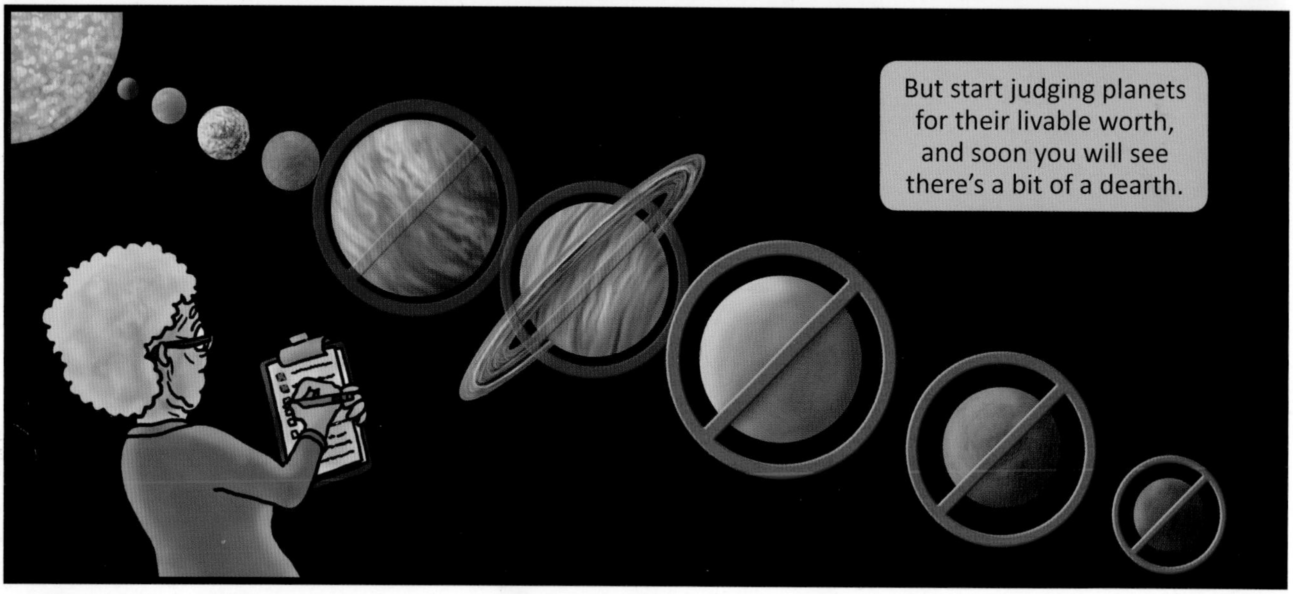
But start judging planets for their livable worth, and soon you will see there's a bit of a dearth.

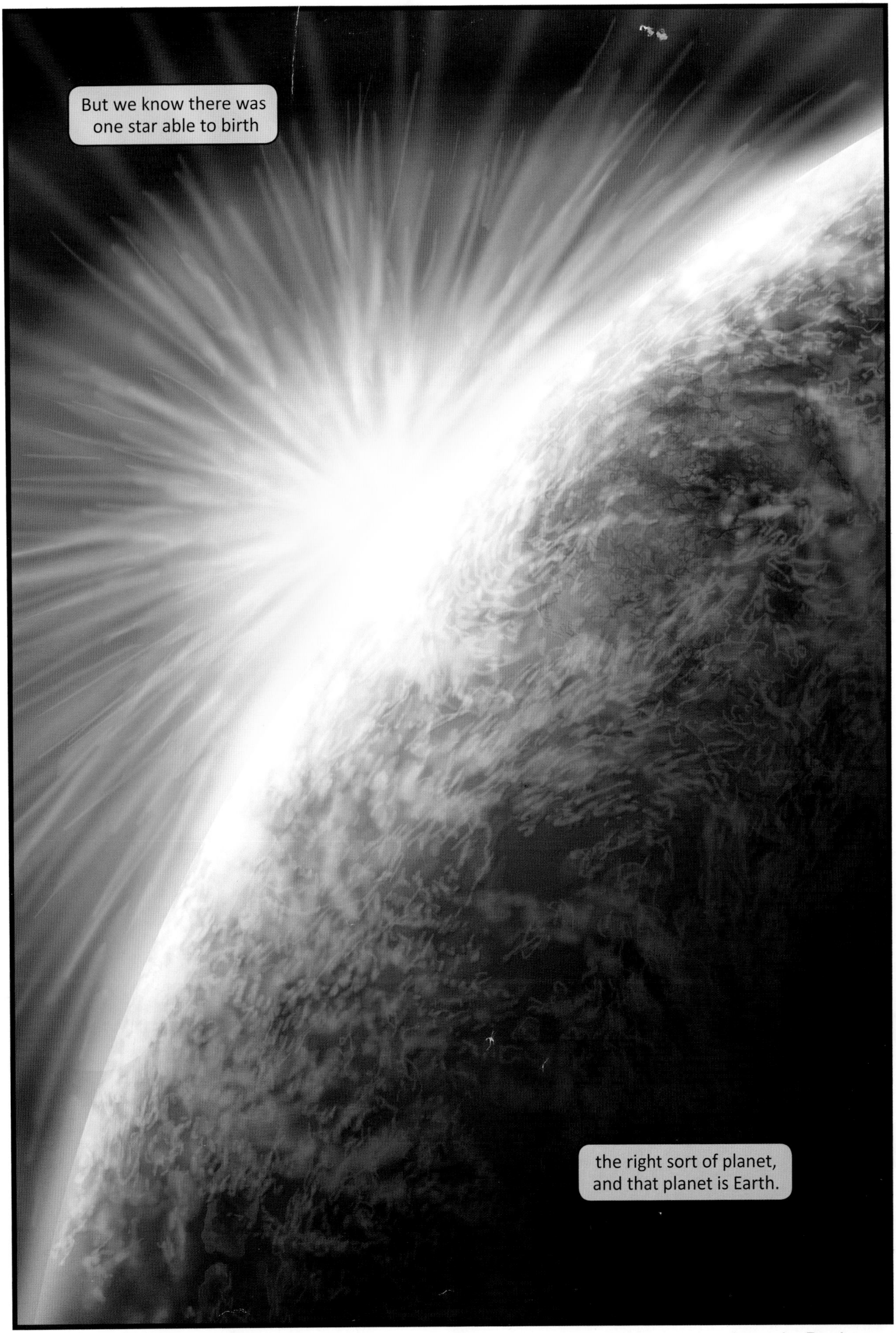
But we know there was one star able to birth
the right sort of planet, and that planet is Earth.

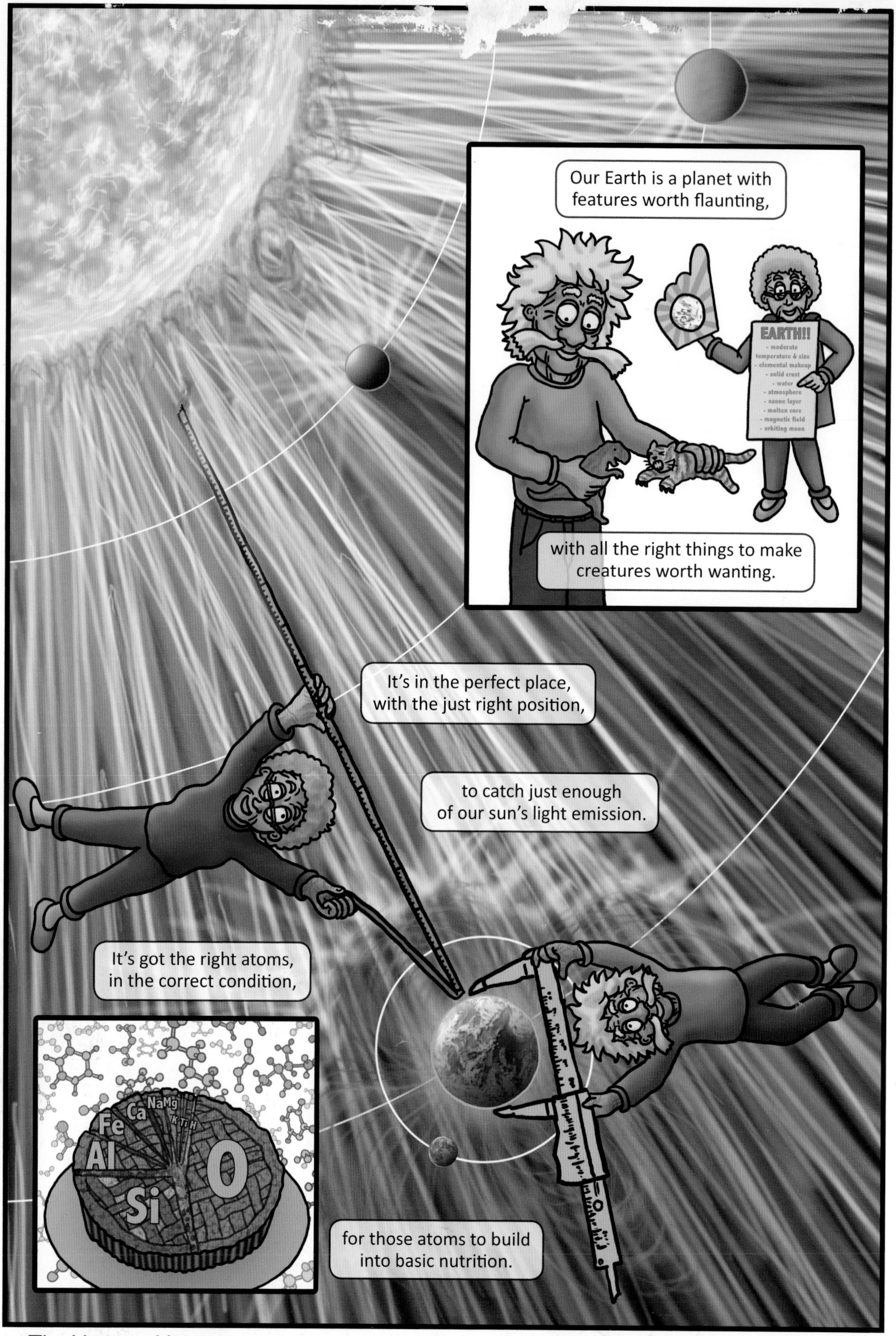
Our Earth is a planet with features worth flaunting,
EARTH!!
- moderate temperature & size
- elemental makeup
- solid crust
- water
- atmosphere
- ozone layer
- molten core
- magnetic field
- orbiting moon
with all the right things to make creatures worth wanting.
It's in the perfect place, with the just right position,
to catch just enough of our sun's light emission.
It's got the right atoms, in the correct condition,
Fe
Ca
Na
Mg
K
Ti
H
Al
Si
O
for those atoms to build into basic nutrition.

But at first the Earth was ugly and mean.

It was nothing compared with today's lively scene.

Nothing was living,

not one measly bean.

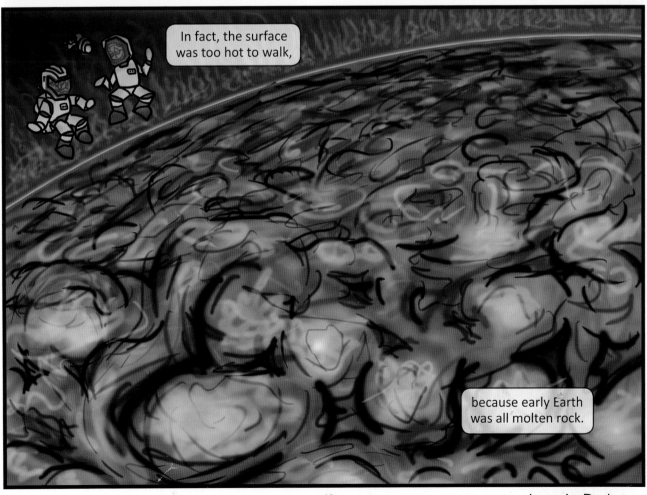

In fact, the surface was too hot to walk,

because early Earth was all molten rock.

James Lu Dunbar

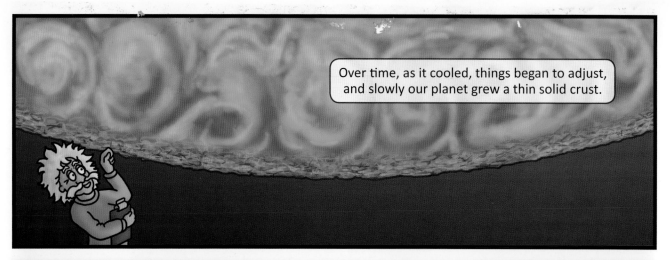

Over time, as it cooled, things began to adjust, and slowly our planet grew a thin solid crust.

The next thing Earth lacked, which it had to develop, was atmospheric gas to protect and envelop.

Gas came to the surface from the inside out,

as volcanoes erupted with many a spout,

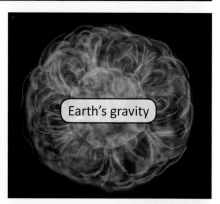

Earth's gravity

kept the gas hanging about.

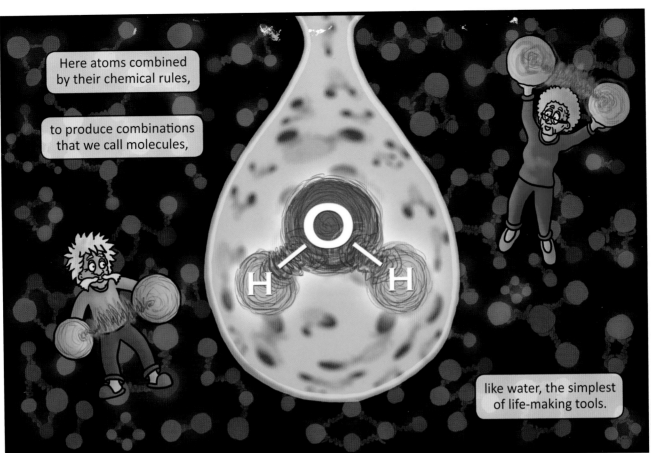

Here atoms combined by their chemical rules,

to produce combinations that we call molecules,

O H H

like water, the simplest of life-making tools.

As the Earth cooled, it started to rain,

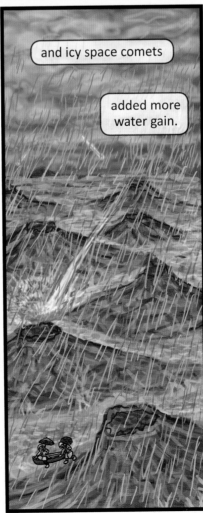

and icy space comets

added more water gain.

The land became flooded,

with nowhere to drain.

James Lu Dunbar

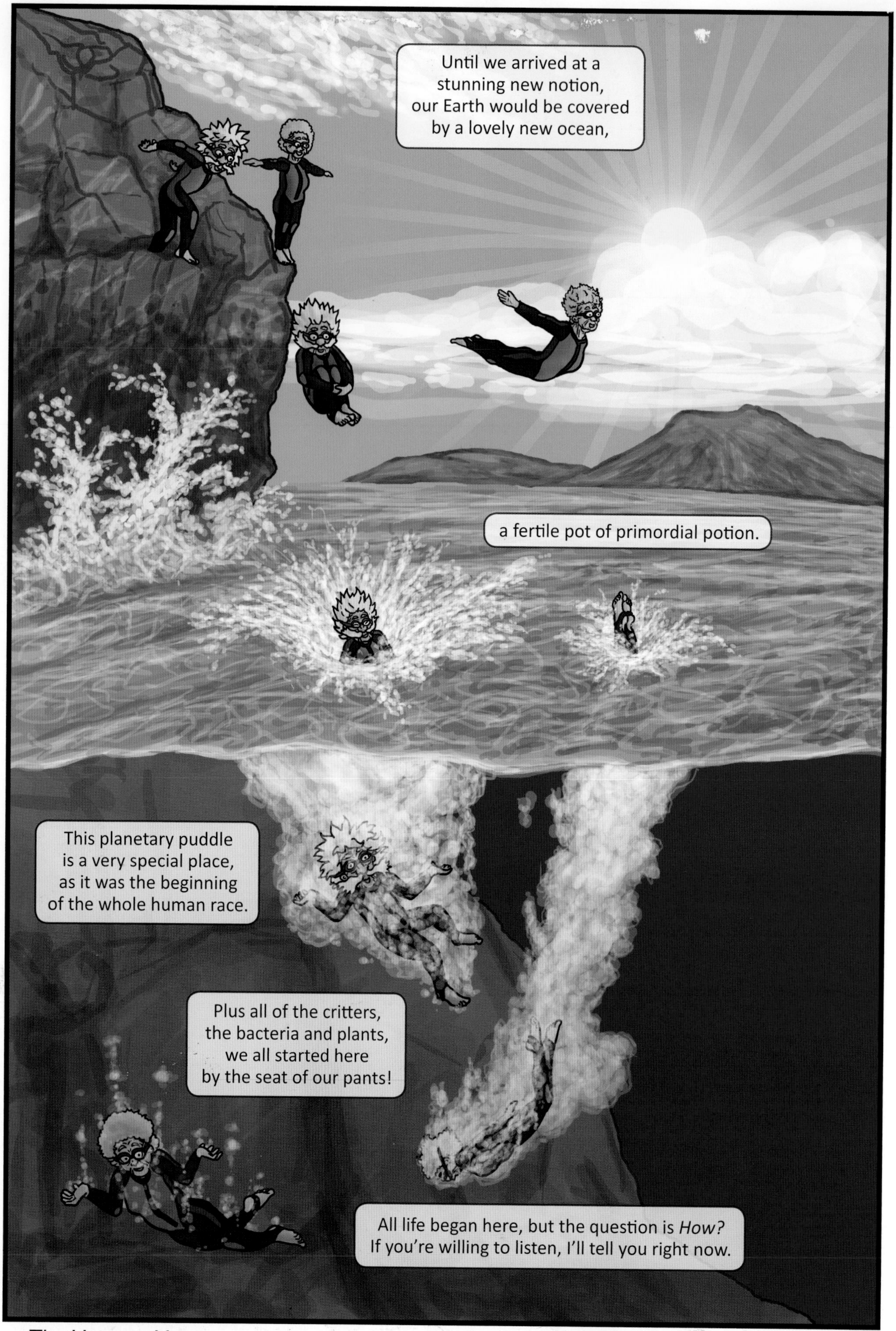
Until we arrived at a stunning new notion, our Earth would be covered by a lovely new ocean,
a fertile pot of primordial potion.
This planetary puddle is a very special place, as it was the beginning of the whole human race.
Plus all of the critters, the bacteria and plants, we all started here by the seat of our pants!
All life began here, but the question is *How?* If you're willing to listen, I'll tell you right now.

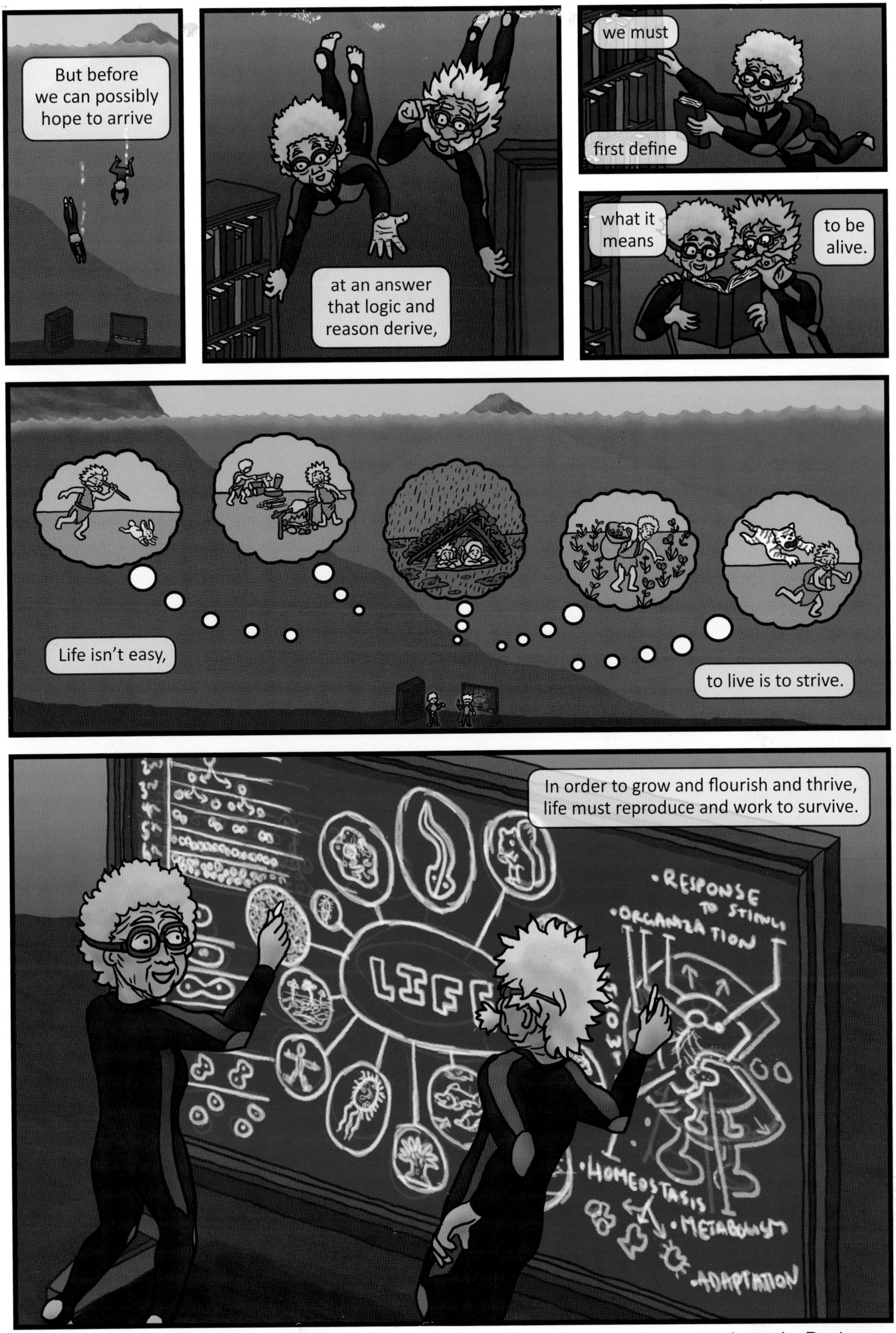
But before we can possibly hope to arrive
at an answer that logic and reason derive,
we must
first define
what it means
to be alive.
Life isn't easy,
to live is to strive.
In order to grow and flourish and thrive,
life must reproduce and work to survive.
LIFE
•RESPONSE TO STIMULI
•ORGANIZATION
•HOMEOSTASIS
•METABOLISM
•ADAPTATION

But exact reproduction is not quite enough,

as it only makes more of just the same stuff.

In order to create life, we need some variation,

when a reproducer makes the next generation.

Mutations prevent the constancy curse,
allowing populations to become more diverse.

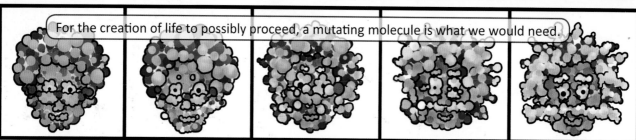

For the creation of life to possibly proceed, a mutating molecule is what we would need.

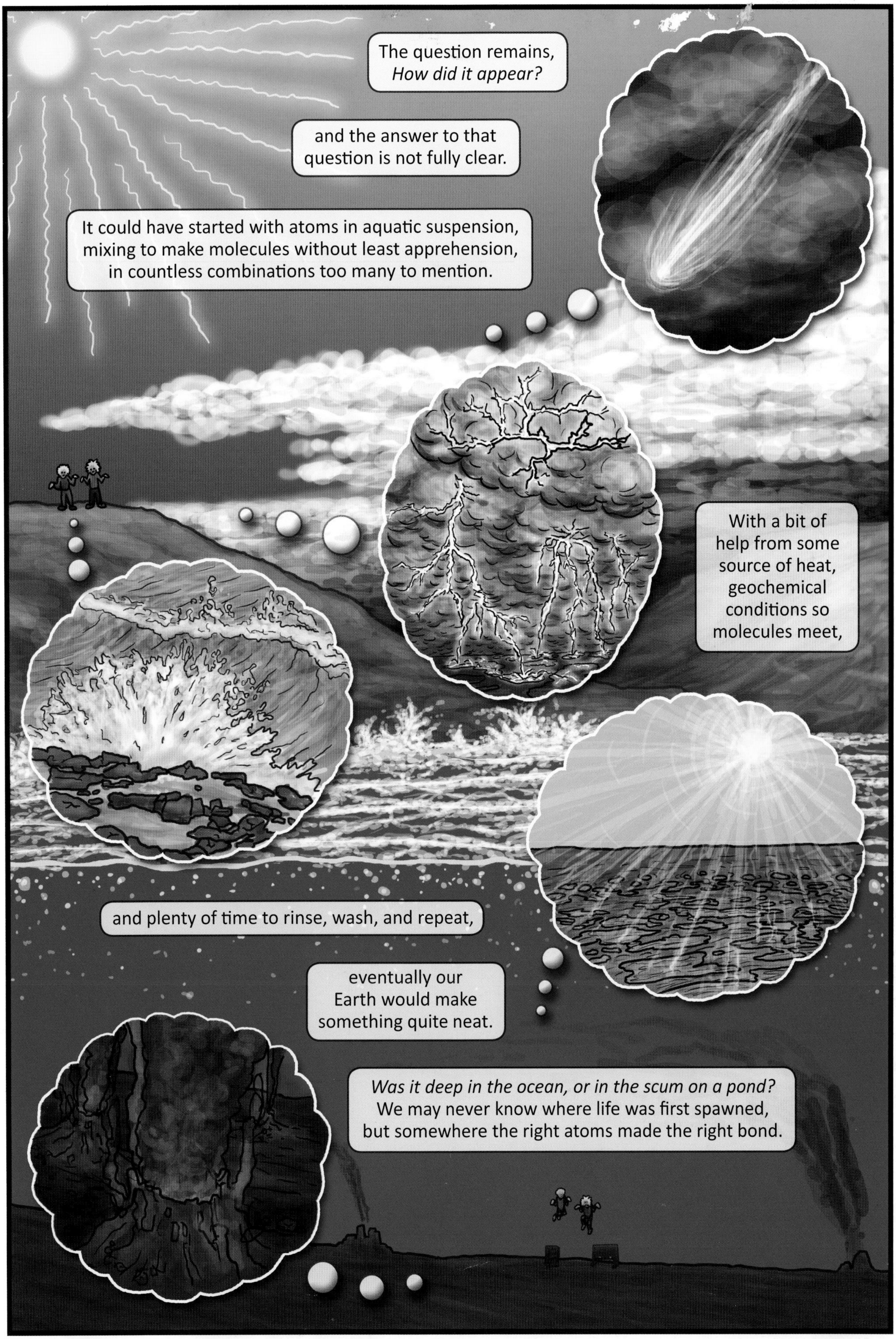
The question remains,
How did it appear?
and the answer to that
question is not fully clear.
It could have started with atoms in aquatic suspension,
mixing to make molecules without least apprehension,
in countless combinations too many to mention.
With a bit of
help from some
source of heat,
geochemical
conditions so
molecules meet,
and plenty of time to rinse, wash, and repeat,
eventually our
Earth would make
something quite neat.
Was it deep in the ocean, or in the scum on a pond?
We may never know where life was first spawned,
but somewhere the right atoms made the right bond.

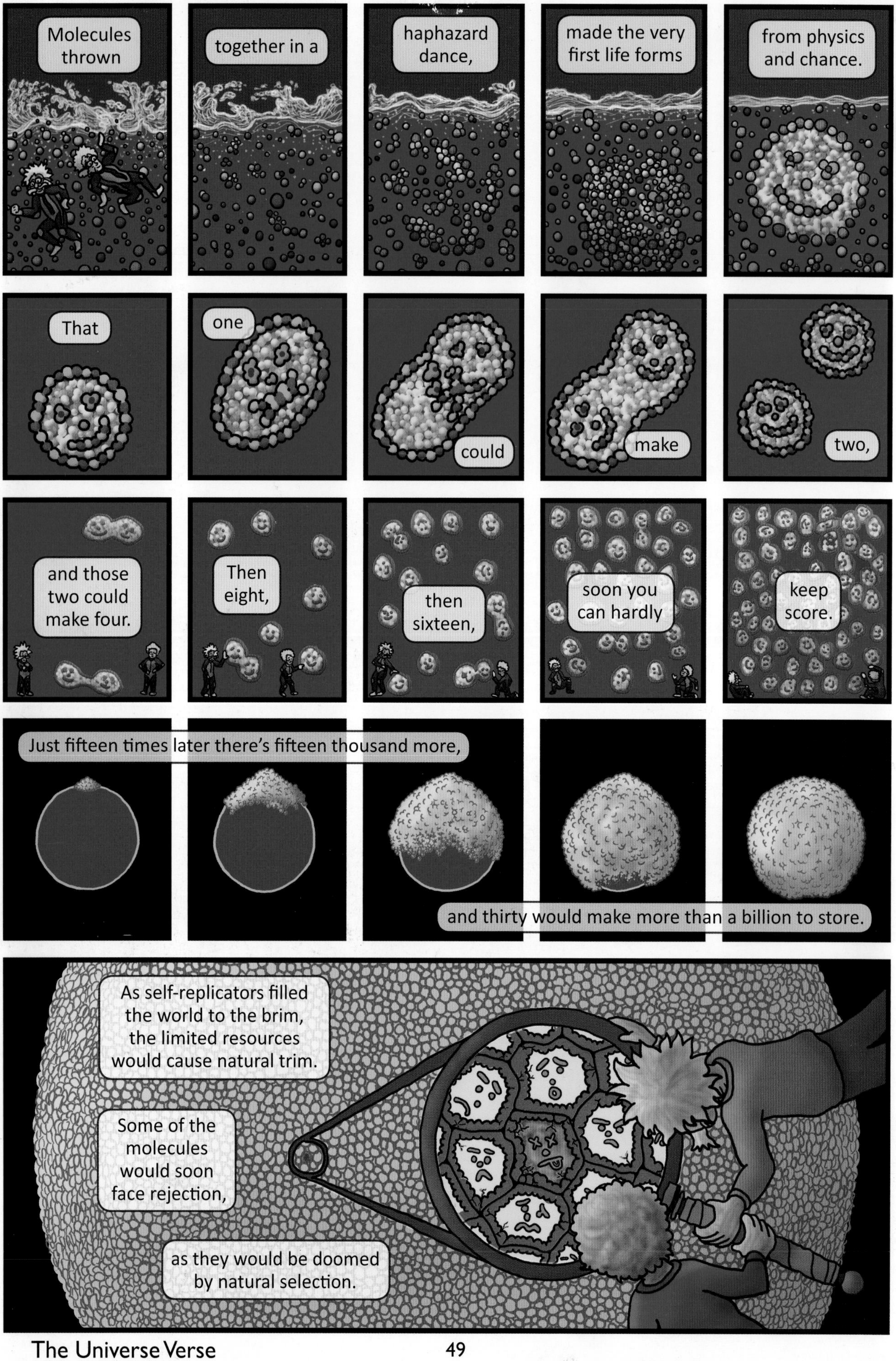
Molecules thrown
together in a
haphazard dance,
made the very first life forms
from physics and chance.
That
one
could
make
two,
and those two could make four.
Then eight,
then sixteen,
soon you can hardly
keep score.
Just fifteen times later there's fifteen thousand more,
and thirty would make more than a billion to store.
As self-replicators filled the world to the brim, the limited resources would cause natural trim.
Some of the molecules would soon face rejection,
as they would be doomed by natural selection.

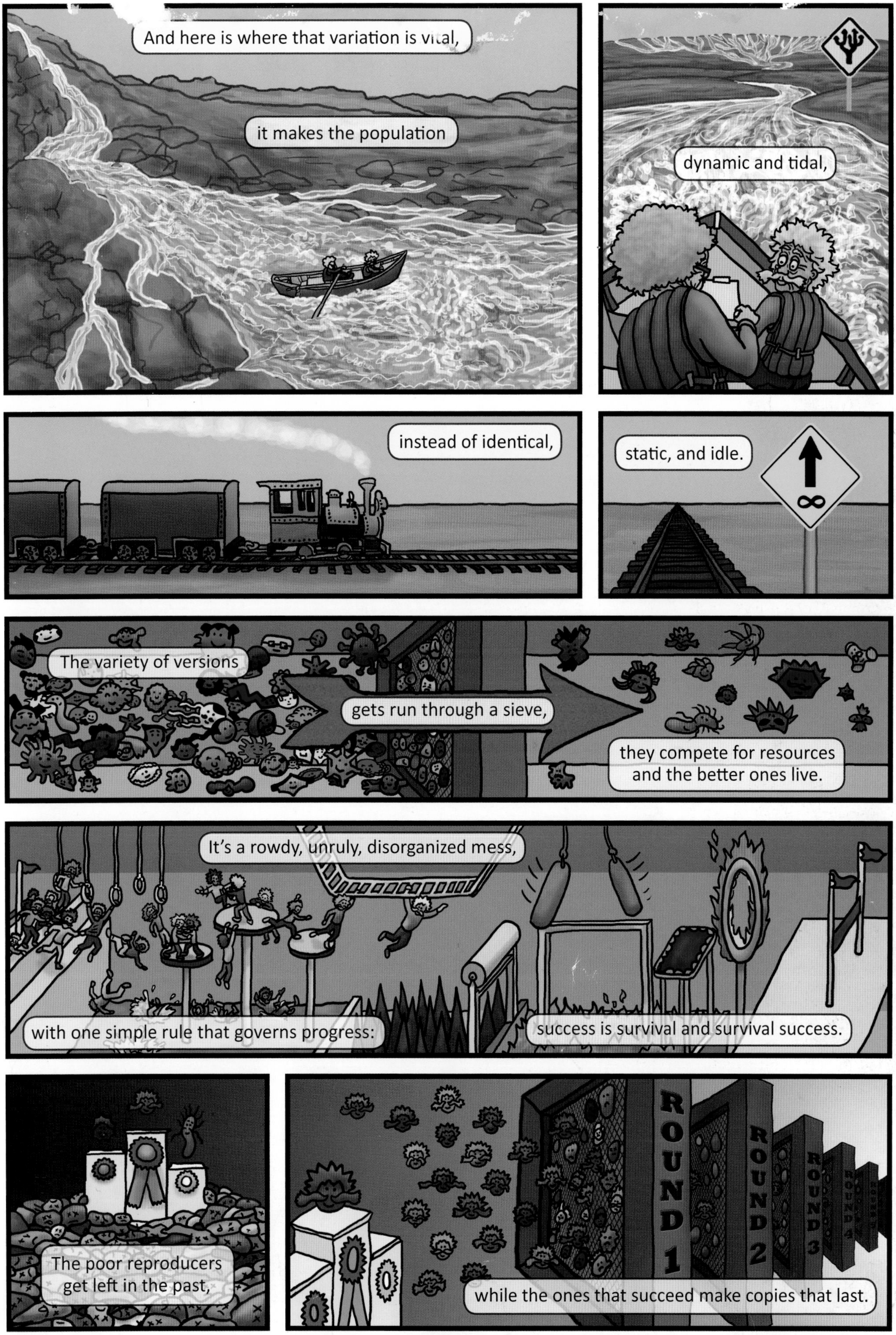
And here is where that variation is vital,
it makes the population
dynamic and tidal,
instead of identical,
static, and idle.
The variety of versions
gets run through a sieve,
they compete for resources and the better ones live.
It's a rowdy, unruly, disorganized mess,
with one simple rule that governs progress:
success is survival and survival success.
The poor reproducers get left in the past,
while the ones that succeed make copies that last.
ROUND 1
ROUND 2
ROUND 3

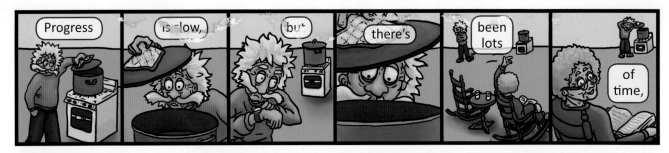

Progress
is slow,
but
there's
been lots
of time,
since our humble beginnings as primitive slime.
For the Planet
- Mix first three ingredients,
kneading throughly
-Let a firm crust form
nd Sulfer
se UV radiation,
or deep-sea hydrothermal vents
- Let cream rise to the top
- Simmer for 2,000,000,000 years
Serve Immediately
Some two billion years with a steady tradition,
of natural and constant cutthroat competition.
It's a beautifully simple and sublime solution,
life made itself through its own evolution.

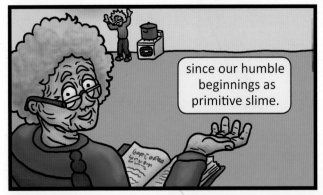

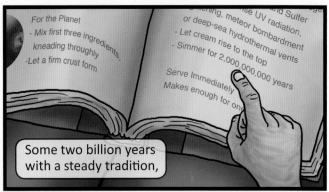

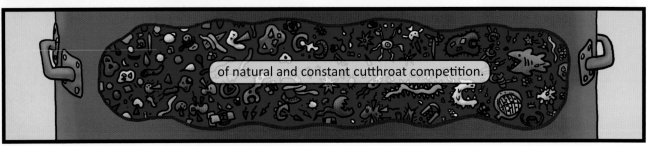

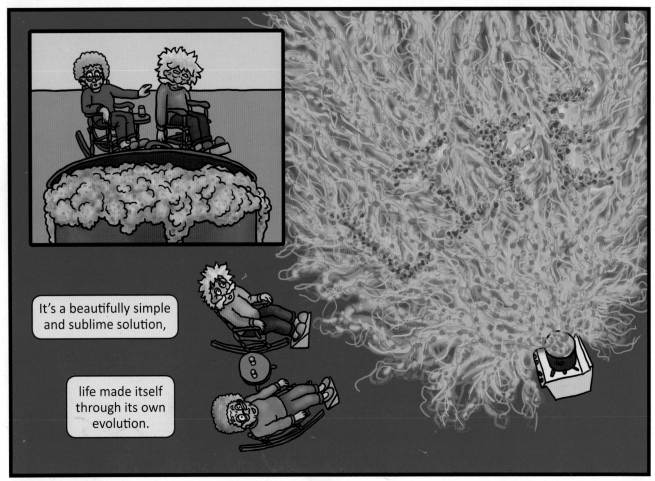

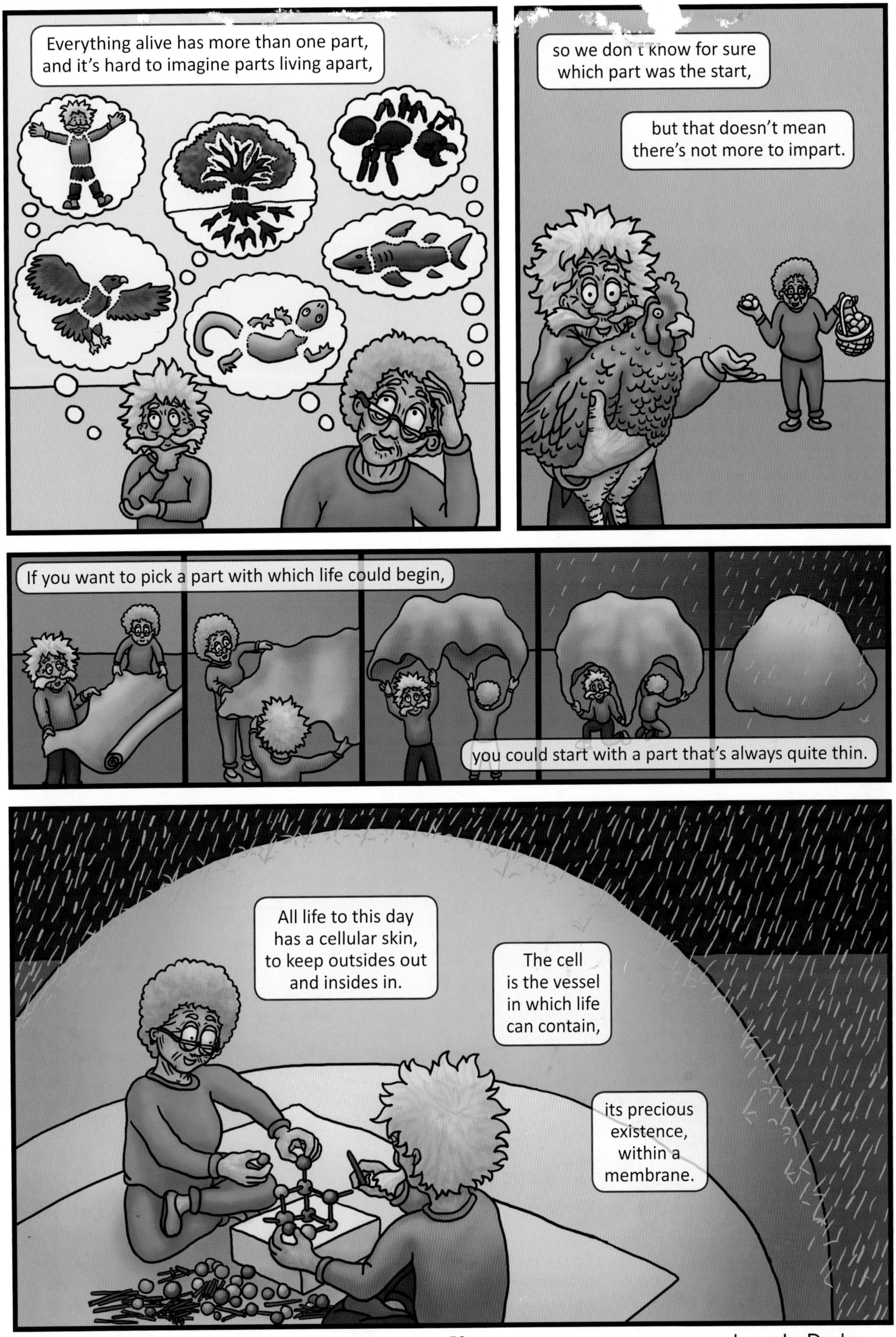
Everything alive has more than one part, and it's hard to imagine parts living apart,
so we don't know for sure which part was the start,
but that doesn't mean there's not more to impart.
If you want to pick a part with which life could begin,
you could start with a part that's always quite thin.
All life to this day has a cellular skin, to keep outsides out and insides in.
The cell is the vessel in which life can contain,
its precious existence, within a membrane.

Inside of its cell new tricks could be tried,

till life chanced upon the first nucleotide.

These bits

are the base

A - T
A - T
C - G
C - G

for a chemical code

that allows information to be easily stowed.

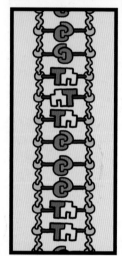

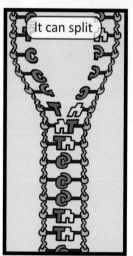

It can split

to make copies

that are very exact,

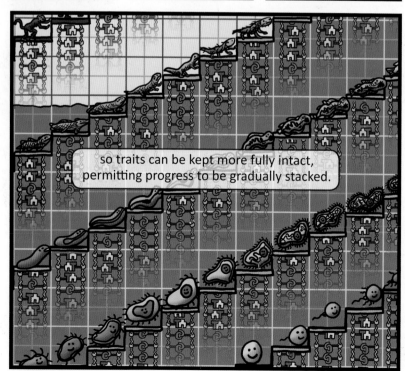

so traits can be kept more fully intact,
permitting progress to be gradually stacked.

Of course, please remember
it could also be reckoned
that this code came first
and the cells came second.

We don't know now
and we may never know,
but somehow it happened,
so on with the show.

The Universe Verse

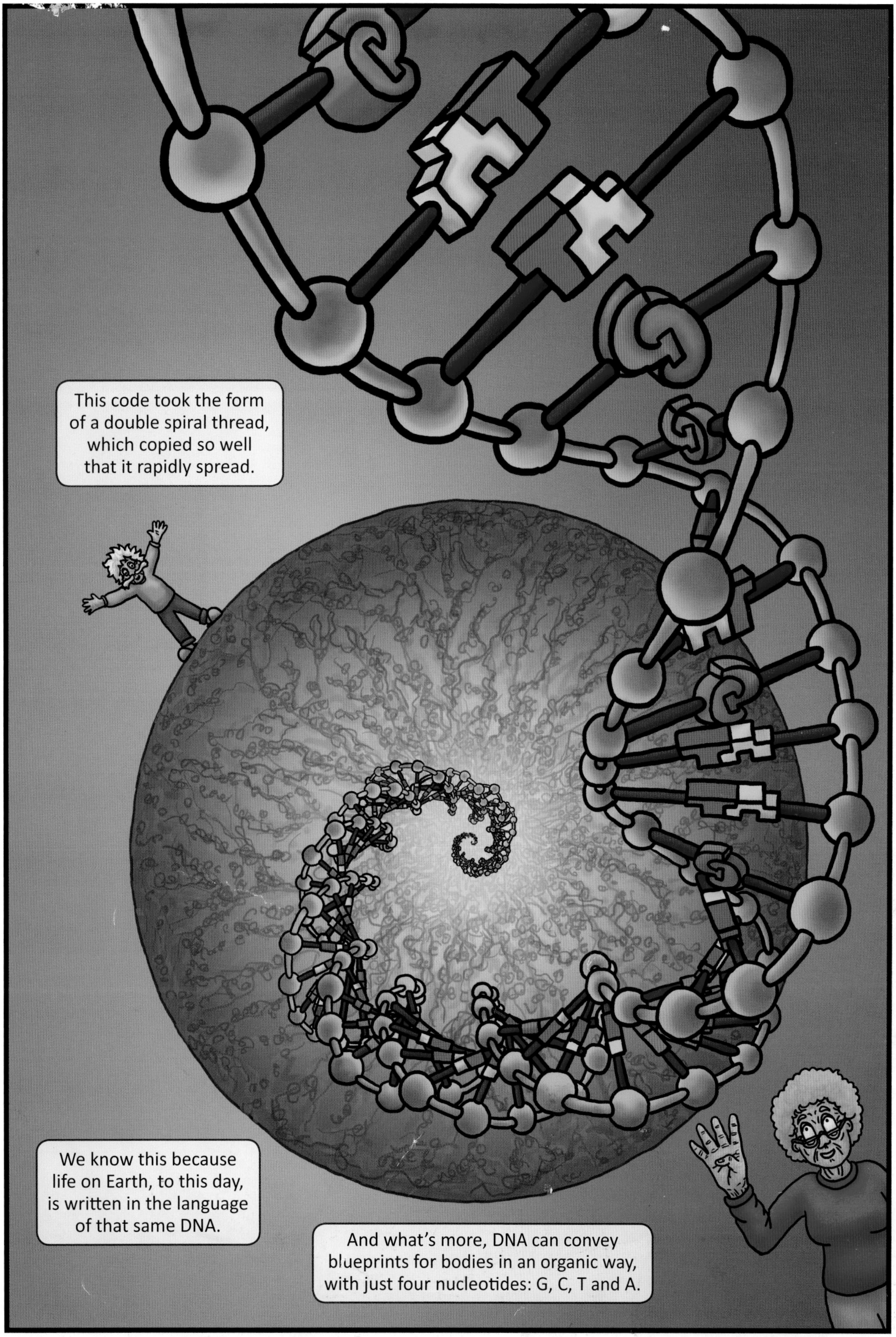
This code took the form of a double spiral thread, which copied so well that it rapidly spread.
We know this because life on Earth, to this day, is written in the language of that same DNA.
And what's more, DNA can convey blueprints for bodies in an organic way, with just four nucleotides: G, C, T and A.

These DNA strands are living instructions, for the creation of creature constructions.

DNA's great power is that it can talk,

as a code for aminos, life's building block.

TAC-GGG-TGA-GGC-ATA-_

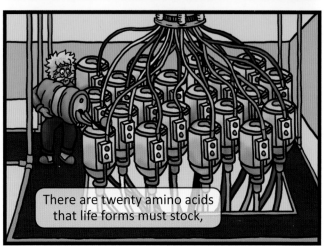

There are twenty amino acids that life forms must stock,

DNA orders them, they fold and interlock.

The resulting structure is called a protein.

They're the pieces and parts of each living machine.

All the DNA that makes one

is part of one gene.

DNA meant life forms

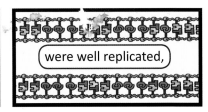

were well replicated,

so life was in danger of becoming stagnated, as less variation was being created.

Evolution, of course, was prepared to get fixing, as this problem would be solved with sexual mixing.

Sex can take place as a gene-swapping trade,

or parents can cooperate so offspring are made.

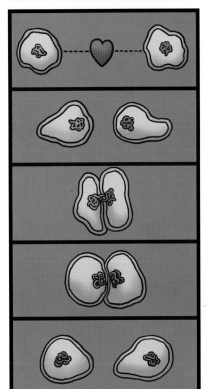

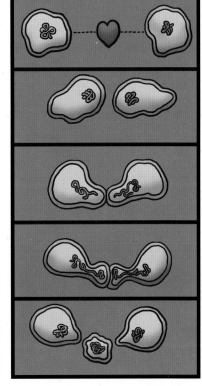

Either way it allows for new gene combinations,

and provides a sure source of routine innovations.

James Lu Dunbar

But the traders can't be too genetically distant,

or the genes that are traded will be inconsistent.

As a result there grew sexual rules,

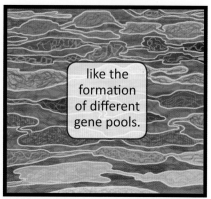

like the formation of different gene pools.

Each pool is a species, a life form distinct, with its own set of genes, that are relatively linked, swapped within a species through sexual instinct.

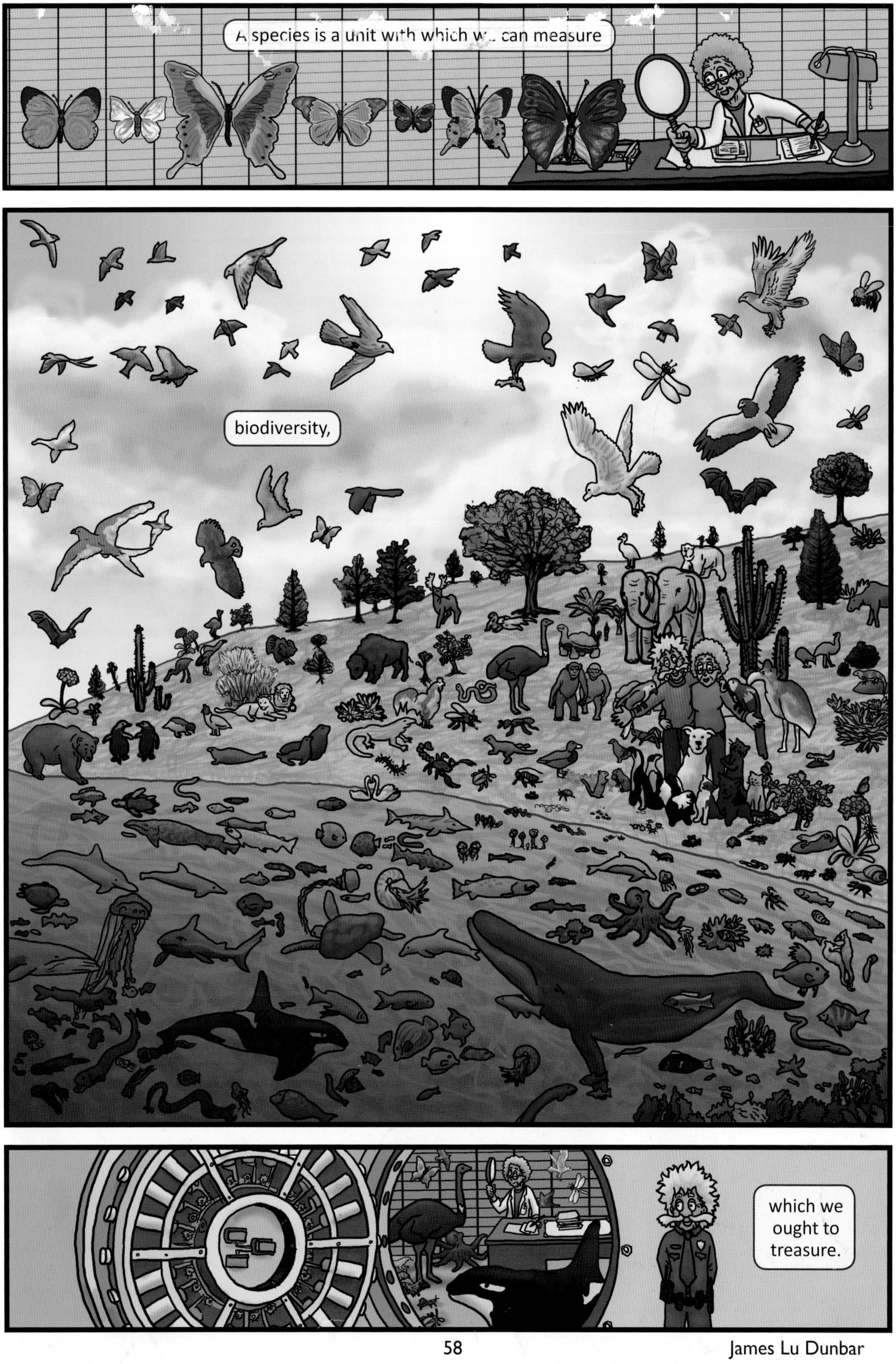
A species is a unit with which we can measure
biodiversity,
which we ought to treasure.

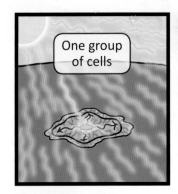

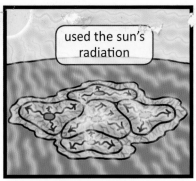

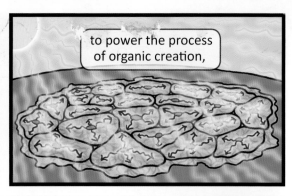

One group of cells
used the sun's radiation
to power the process of organic creation,
CO_2
O_2
using photosynthetic food generation.
H_2O
$2H_2O + 2NADP^+ + 3ADP +$
+ SUNLIGHT
This series of reactions can harness the sun,
$SUNLIGHT + 6H_2O + 6CO_2$
$2NADPH + 2H^+$
ATP
NADPH
RuBP
$+6NADPH$
$+6H^+$
phosphate
$6O_2 + C_6H_{12}O_6$
creating the fuel on which we all run.
These cells spread out in a great green bloom, filling the oceans, they crowded for room,
turning light into food other cells could consume.

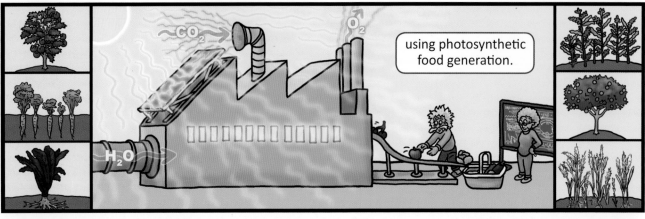

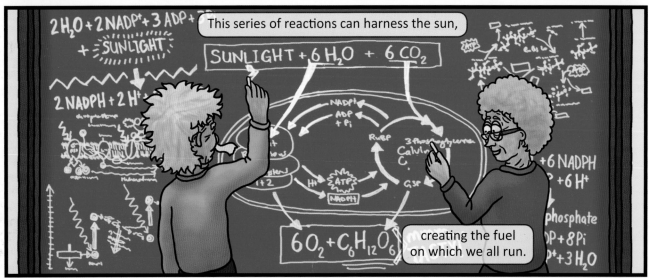

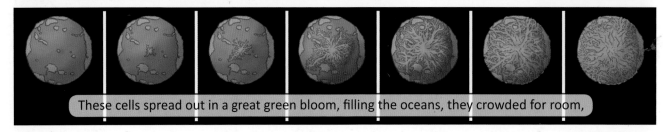

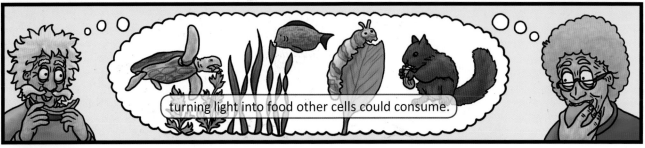

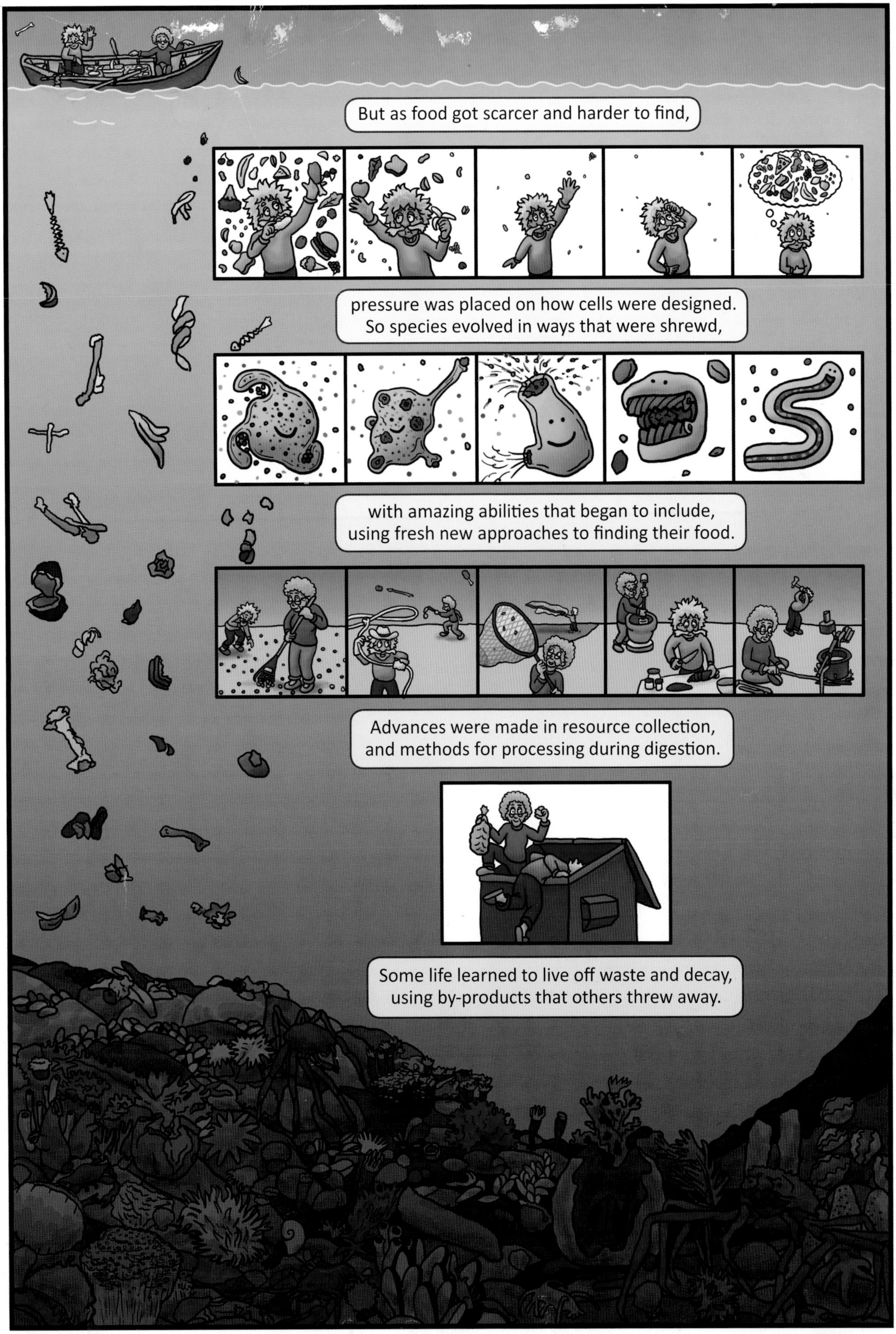
But as food got scarcer and harder to find,
pressure was placed on how cells were designed.
So species evolved in ways that were shrewd,
with amazing abilities that began to include,
using fresh new approaches to finding their food.
Advances were made in resource collection,
and methods for processing during digestion.
Some life learned to live off waste and decay,
using by-products that others threw away.

…e pressure was on, evolution would rem… … …orm that failed to improve,

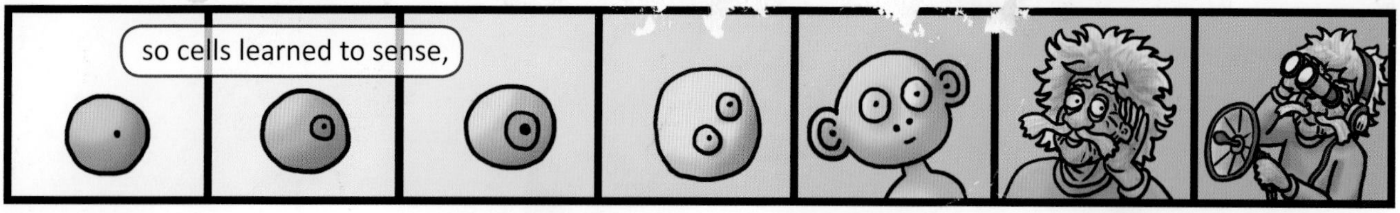
so cells learned to sense,

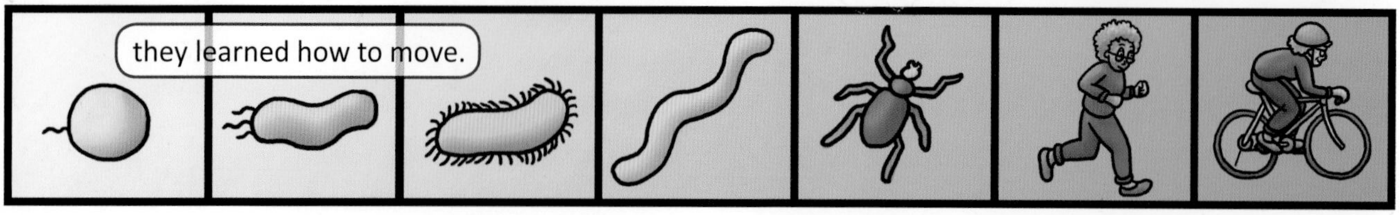
they learned how to move.

Each cell advanced along its own front, as some cells evolved into ones that would hunt.

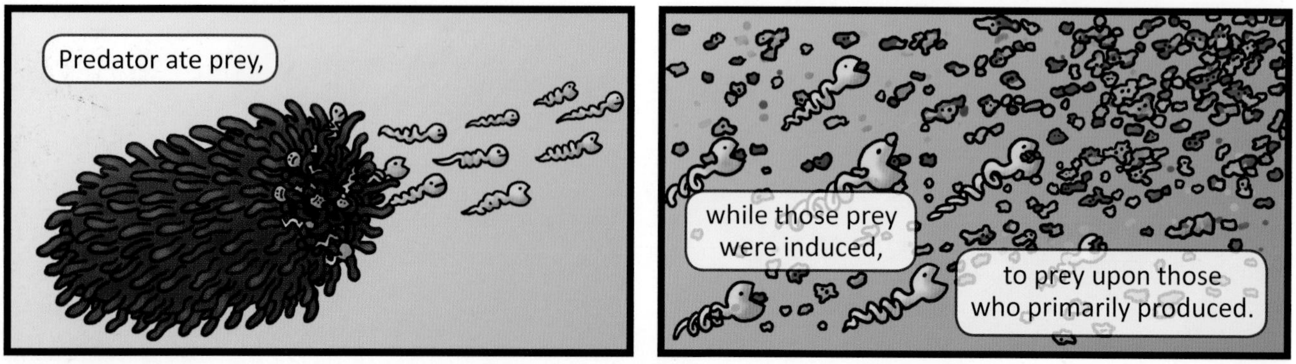
Predator ate prey,
while those prey were induced,
to prey upon those who primarily produced.

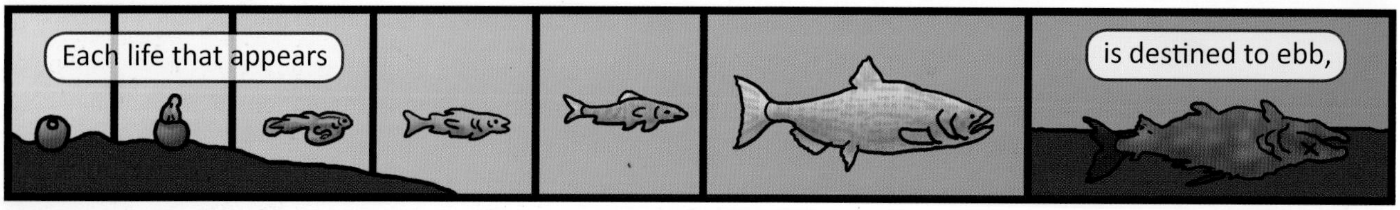
Each life that appears
is destined to ebb,

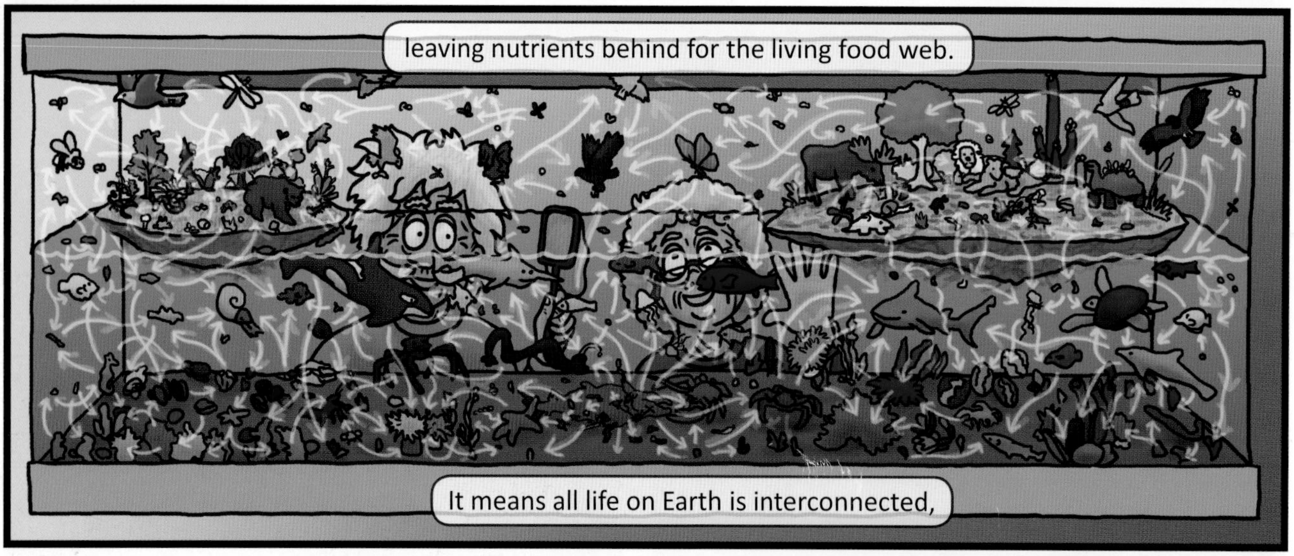
leaving nutrients behind for the living food web.
It means all life on Earth is interconnected,

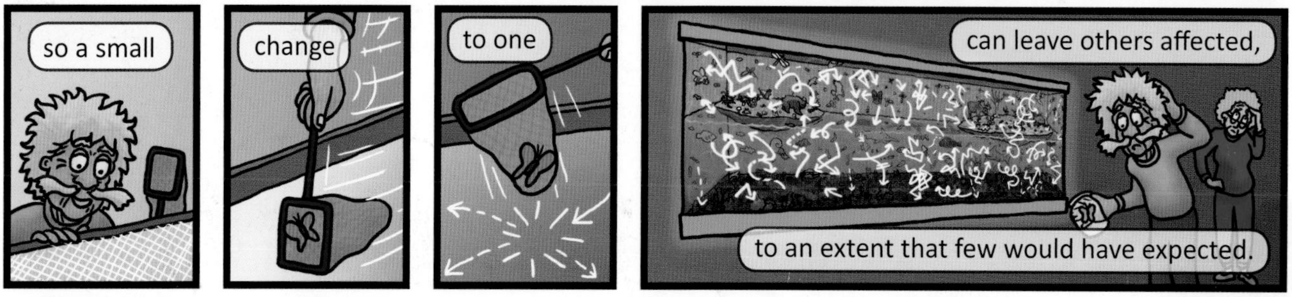
so a small
change
to one
can leave others affected,
to an extent that few would have expected.

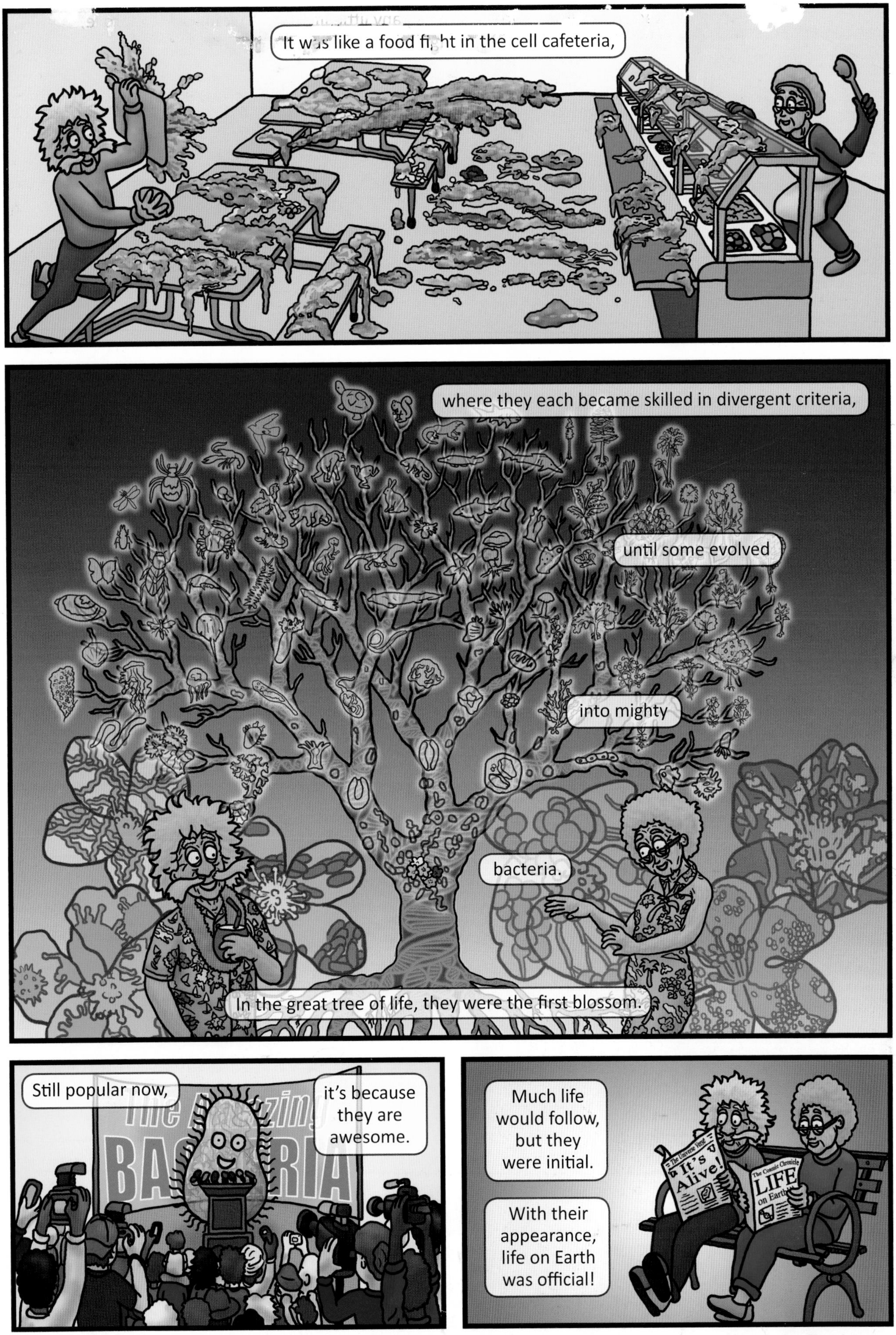
It was like a food fi ht in the cell cafeteria,
where they each became skilled in divergent criteria,
until some evolved
into mighty
bacteria.
In the great tree of life, they were the first blossom.
Still popular now,
it's because they are awesome.
Much life would follow, but they were initial.
With their appearance, life on Earth was official!
It's Alive!
LIFE on Earth

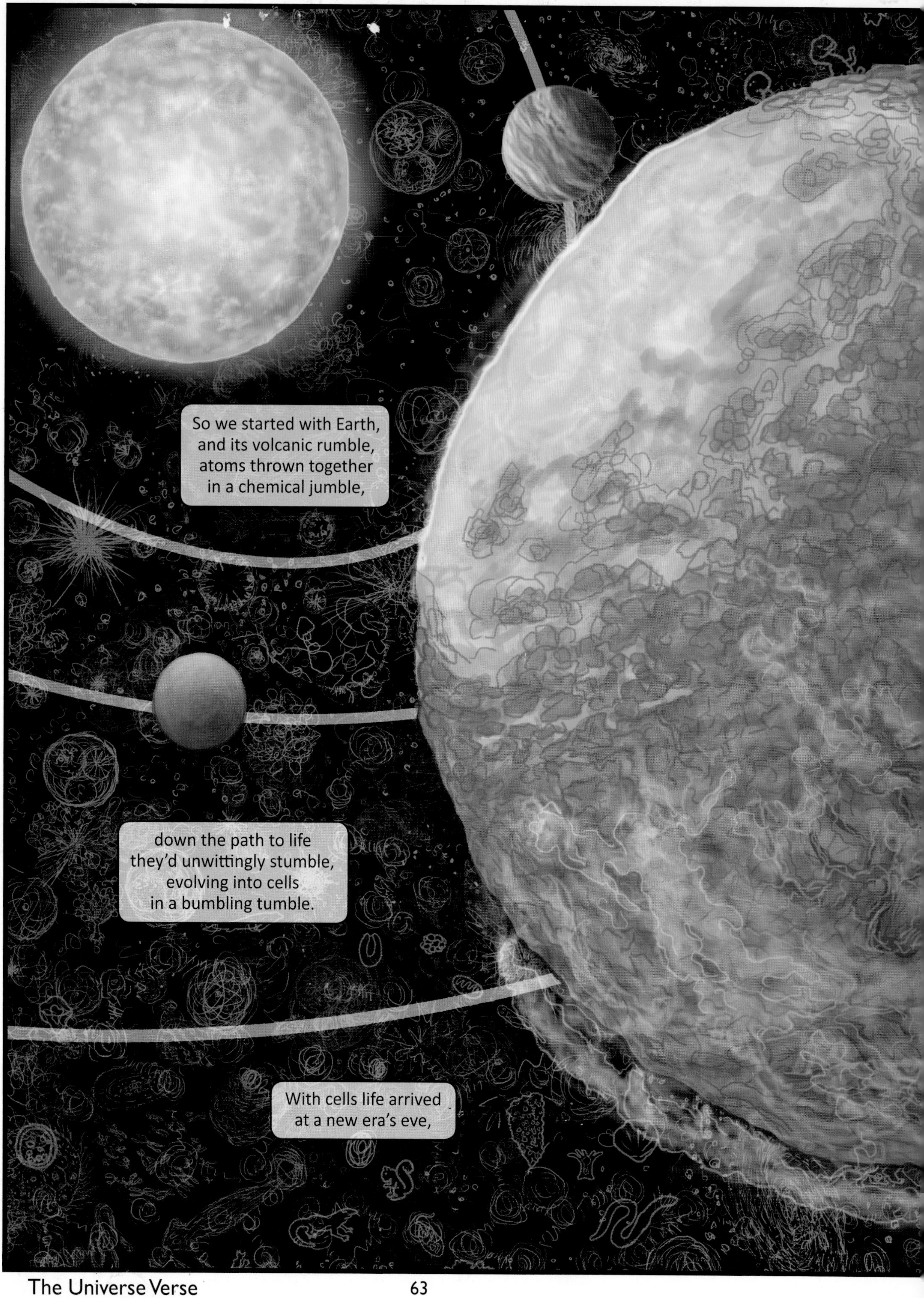
So we started with Earth,
and its volcanic rumble,
atoms thrown together
in a chemical jumble,
down the path to life
they'd unwittingly stumble,
evolving into cells
in a bumbling tumble.
With cells life arrived
at a new era's eve,

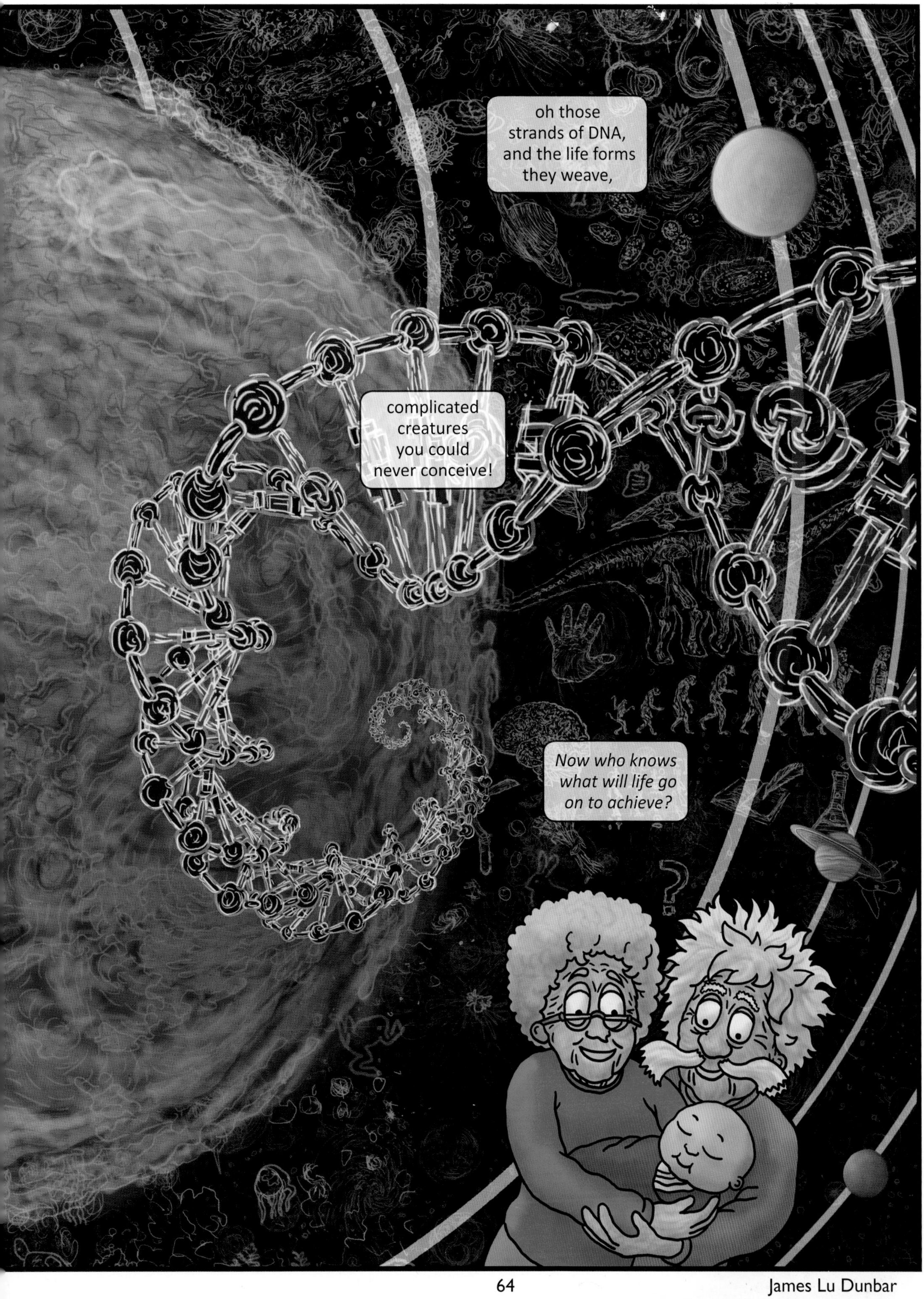
oh those strands of DNA, and the life forms they weave,
complicated creatures you could never conceive!
Now who knows what will life go on to achieve?

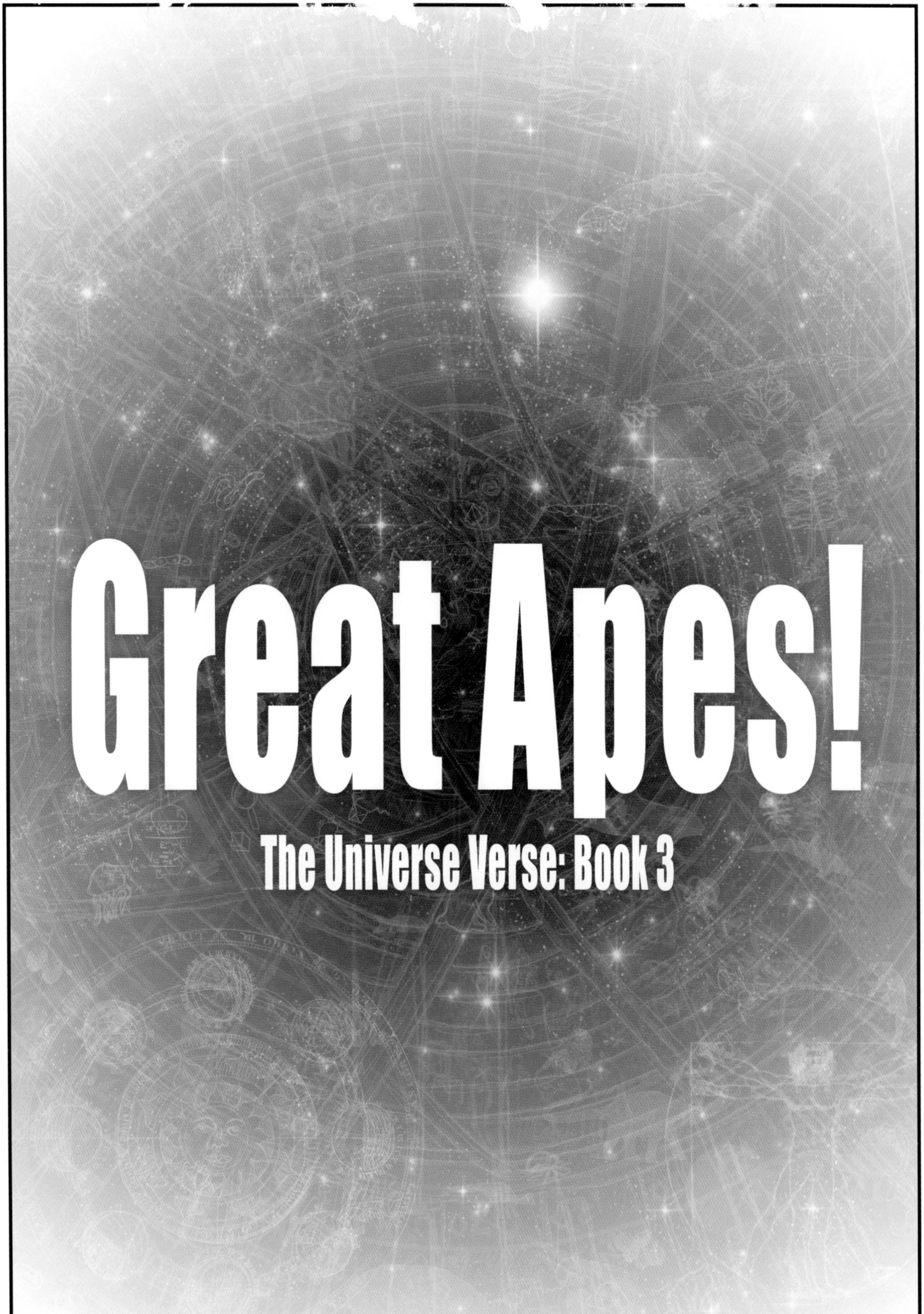

Great Apes!

The Universe Verse: Book 3

We are a way for the cosmos to know itself.

- Carl Sagan

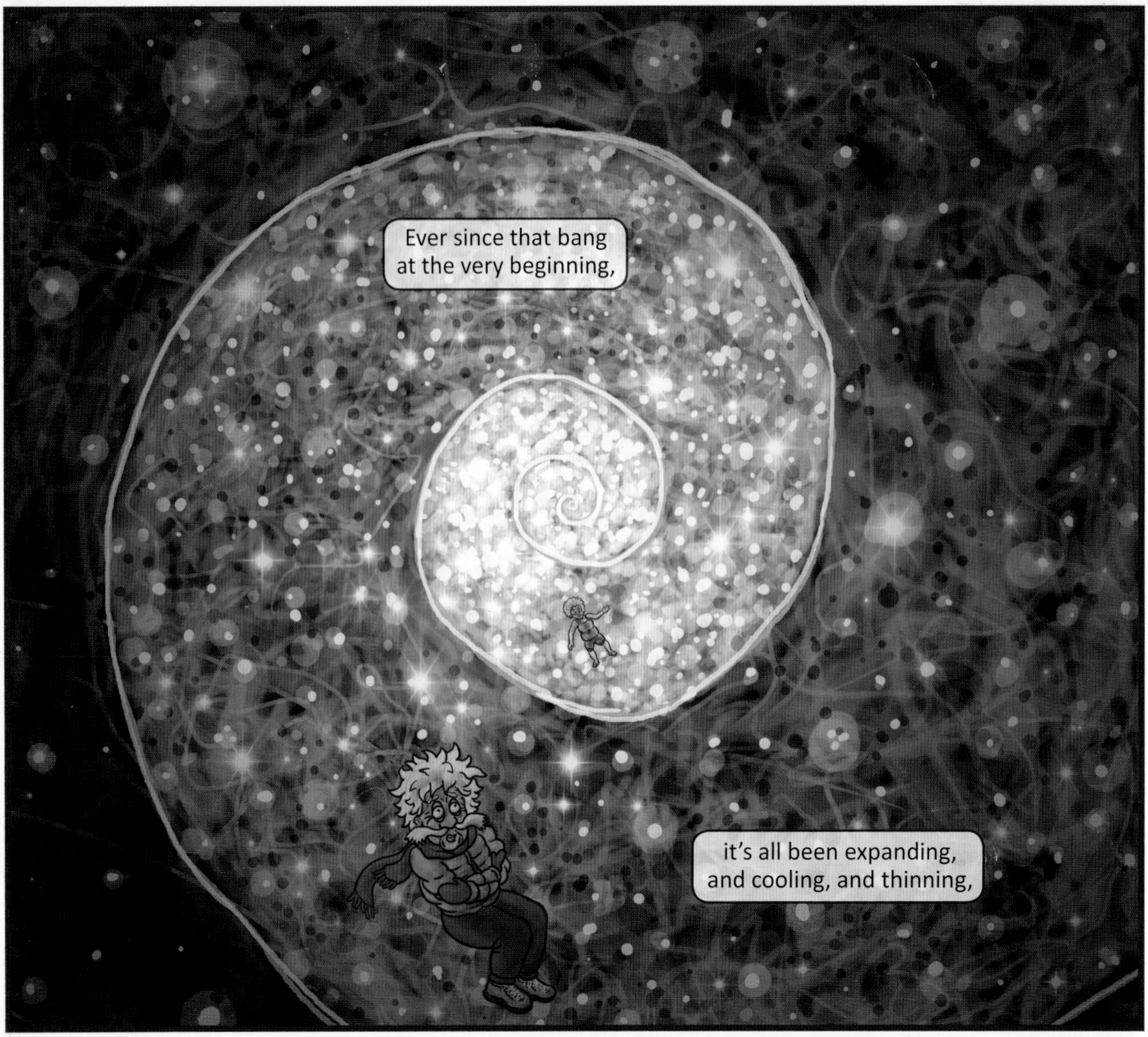
Ever since that bang
at the very beginning,
it's all been expanding,
and cooling, and thinning,

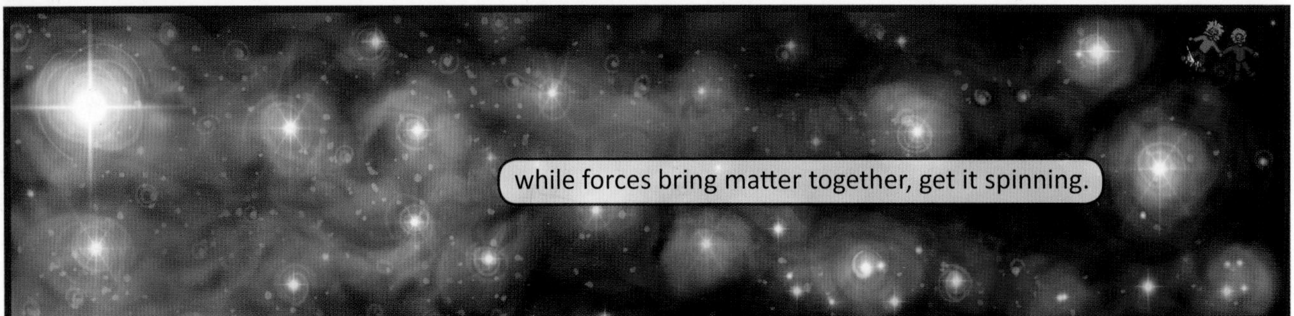
while forces bring matter together, get it spinning.

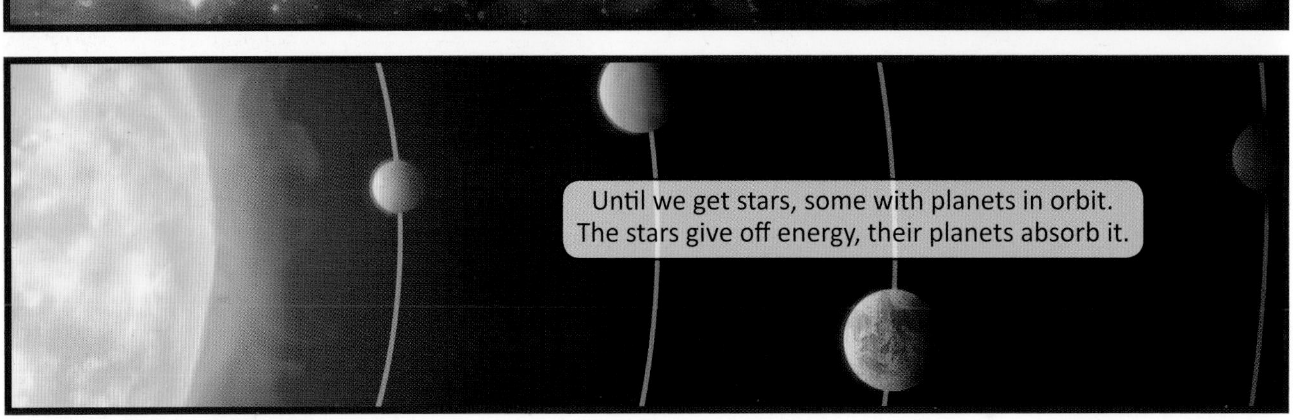
Until we get stars, some with planets in orbit.
The stars give off energy, their planets absorb it.

One of those planets was specially blessed, with comfy conditions lacked by the rest.

Watery and warm with time to invest,

it made some structures of special interest.

Cells with the power to grow and divide,

they created new forms as they multiplied.

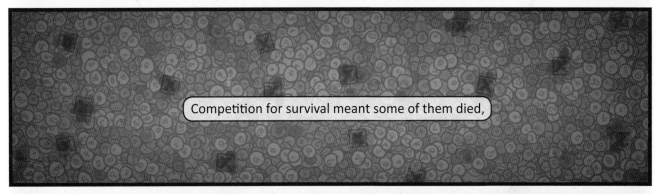

Competition for survival meant some of them died,

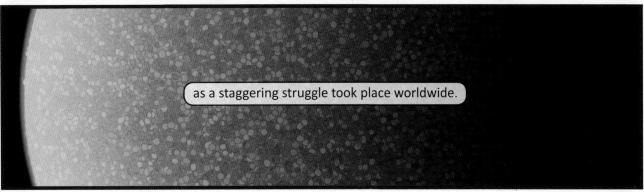

as a staggering struggle took place worldwide.

James Lu Dunbar

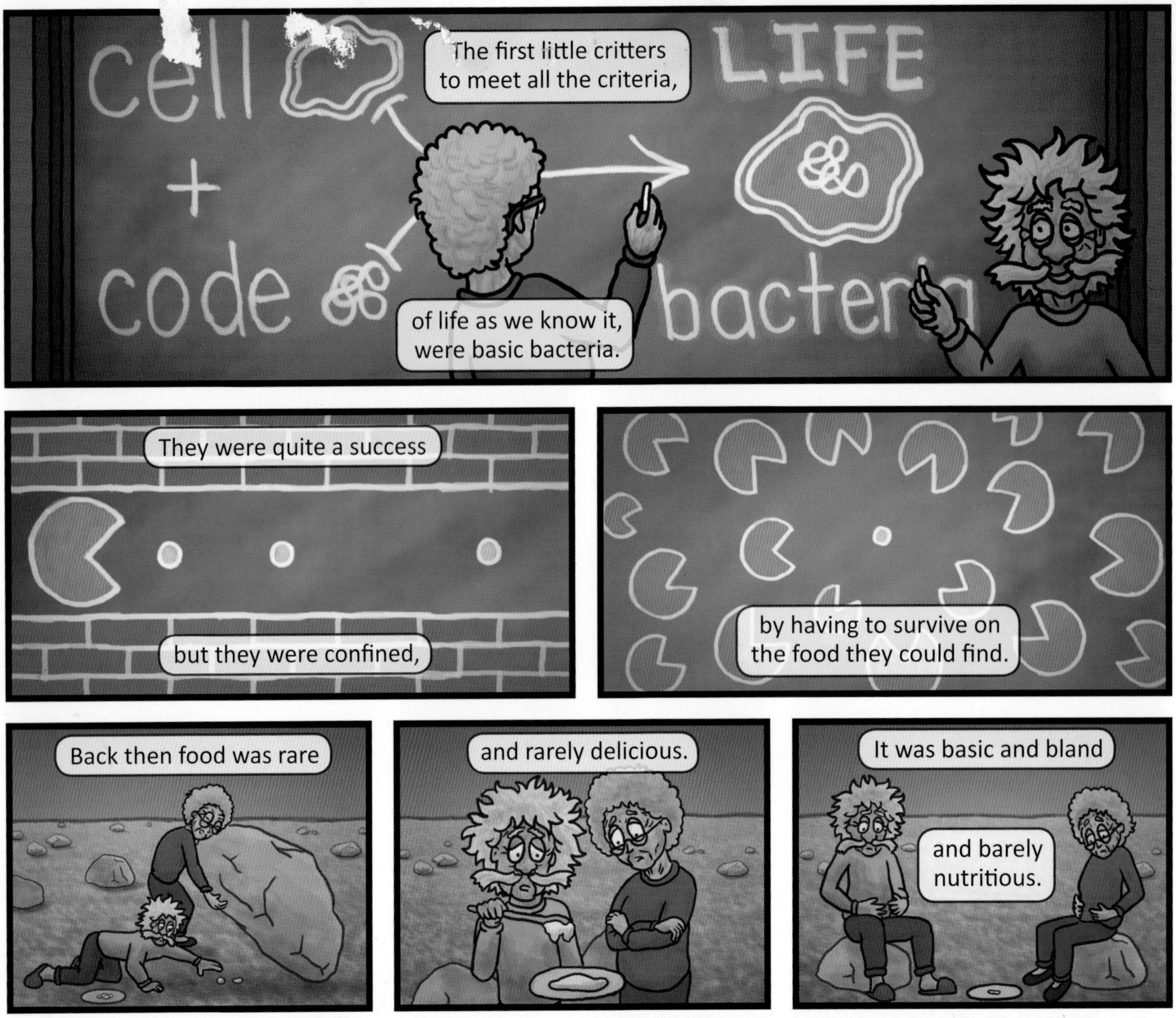
cell
+
code
LIFE
The first little critters to meet all the criteria,
of life as we know it, were basic bacteria.
They were quite a success
but they were confined,
by having to survive on the food they could find.
Back then food was rare
and rarely delicious.
It was basic and bland
and barely nutritious.

And so life would move slowly, at a near standstill, till it unlocked the power of chlorophyll.

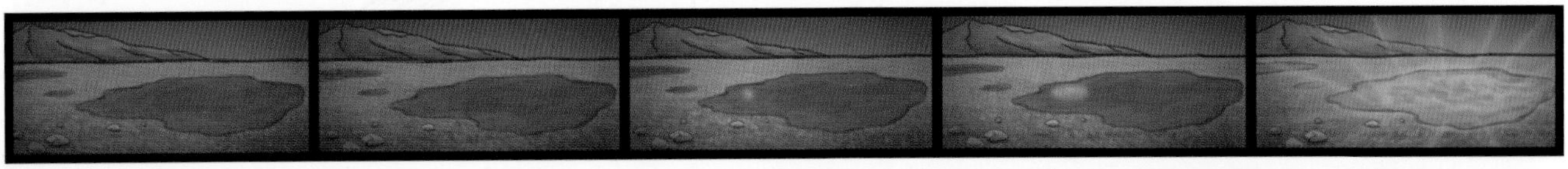

This magical molecule is able to ensnare, raw matter and energy that are present everywhere.

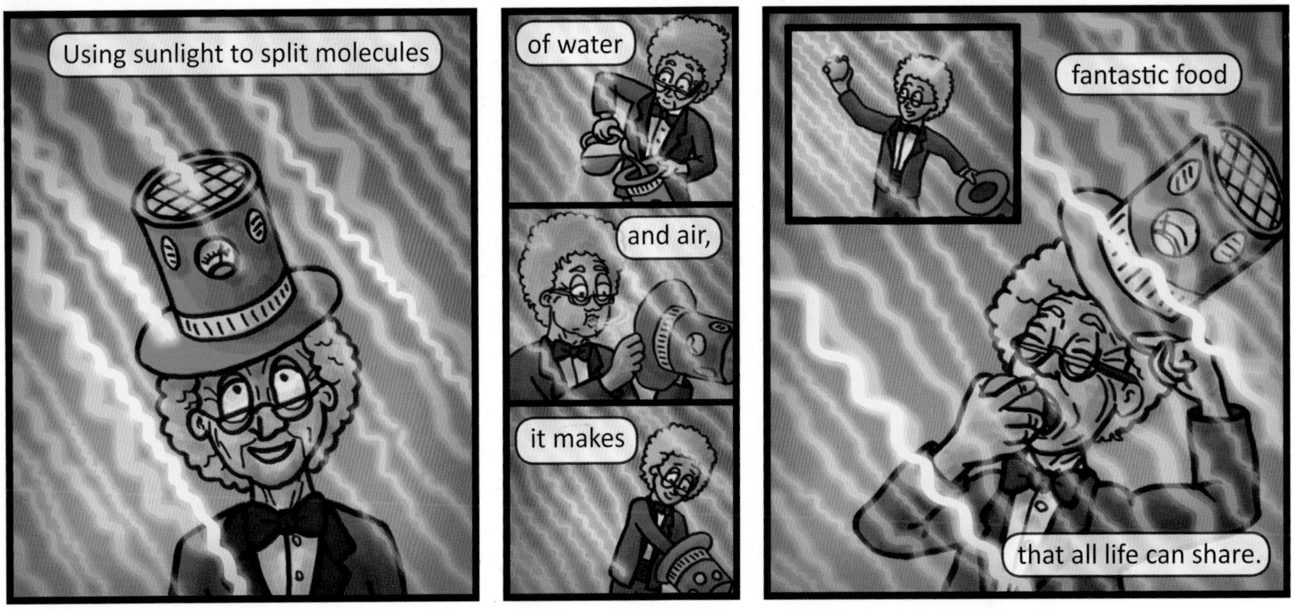
Using sunlight to split molecules
of water
and air,
it makes
fantastic food
that all life can share.

Cells that had it could make food from scratch,

which they did to no end, not aware of the catch.

Photosynthesis makes food

but in the very same turn, it produces a gas

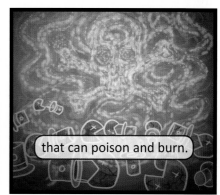

that can poison and burn.

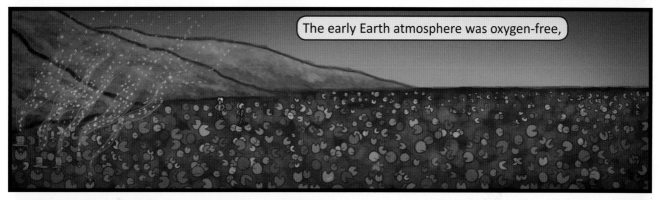

The early Earth atmosphere was oxygen-free,

but the oxygen gas from this food-making spree,

resulted in a rise in toxicity, that caused most bacteria to perish or flee.

James Lu Dunbar

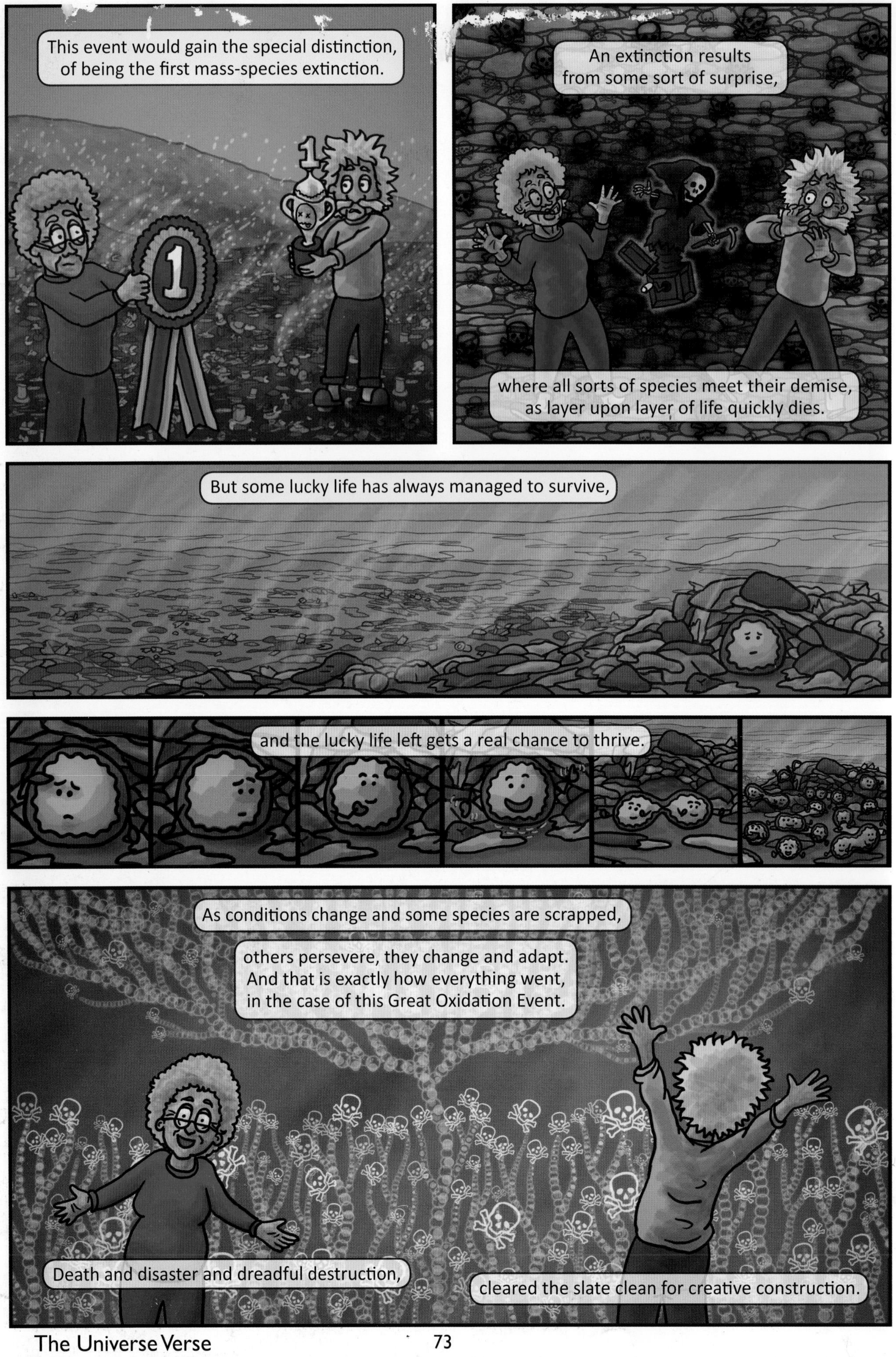
This event would gain the special distinction,
of being the first mass-species extinction.
An extinction results
from some sort of surprise,
where all sorts of species meet their demise,
as layer upon layer of life quickly dies.
But some lucky life has always managed to survive,
and the lucky life left gets a real chance to thrive.
As conditions change and some species are scrapped,
others persevere, they change and adapt.
And that is exactly how everything went,
in the case of this Great Oxidation Event.
Death and disaster and dreadful destruction,
cleared the slate clean for creative construction.

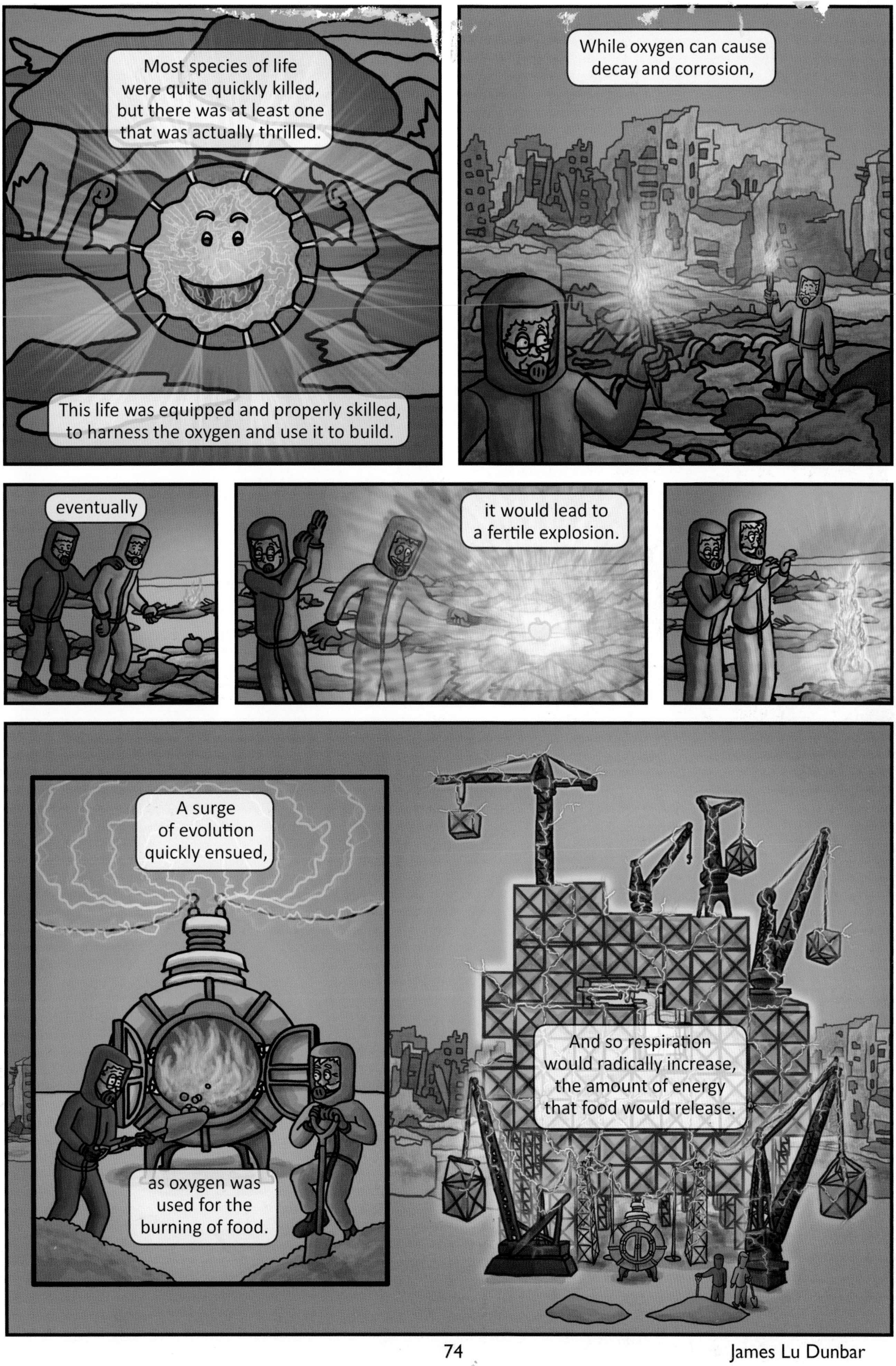

Most species of life were quite quickly killed, but there was at least one that was actually thrilled.
This life was equipped and properly skilled, to harness the oxygen and use it to build.
While oxygen can cause decay and corrosion,
eventually
it would lead to a fertile explosion.
A surge of evolution quickly ensued,
as oxygen was used for the burning of food.
And so respiration would radically increase, the amount of energy that food would release.

This fueled a new creature, complex and exotic, a new type of cell that was eukaryotic.

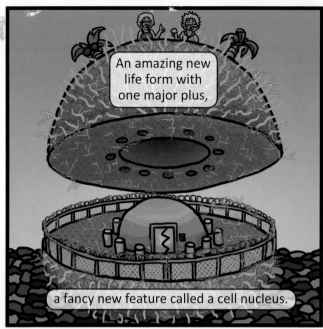

An amazing new life form with one major plus,

a fancy new feature called a cell nucleus.

It's a place

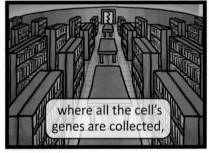

where all the cell's genes are collected,

kept organized, and safely protected.

Now many more genes could be tightly packed, and their various products could then interact. New gene combinations would quickly enhance, the speed at which these cells did advance.

Using the power of evolving genes, life started making new micro machines.

They handle a number of critical deeds, doing the things that every cell needs:

one to cut proteins,

another to paste,

some to store food,

while others take waste.

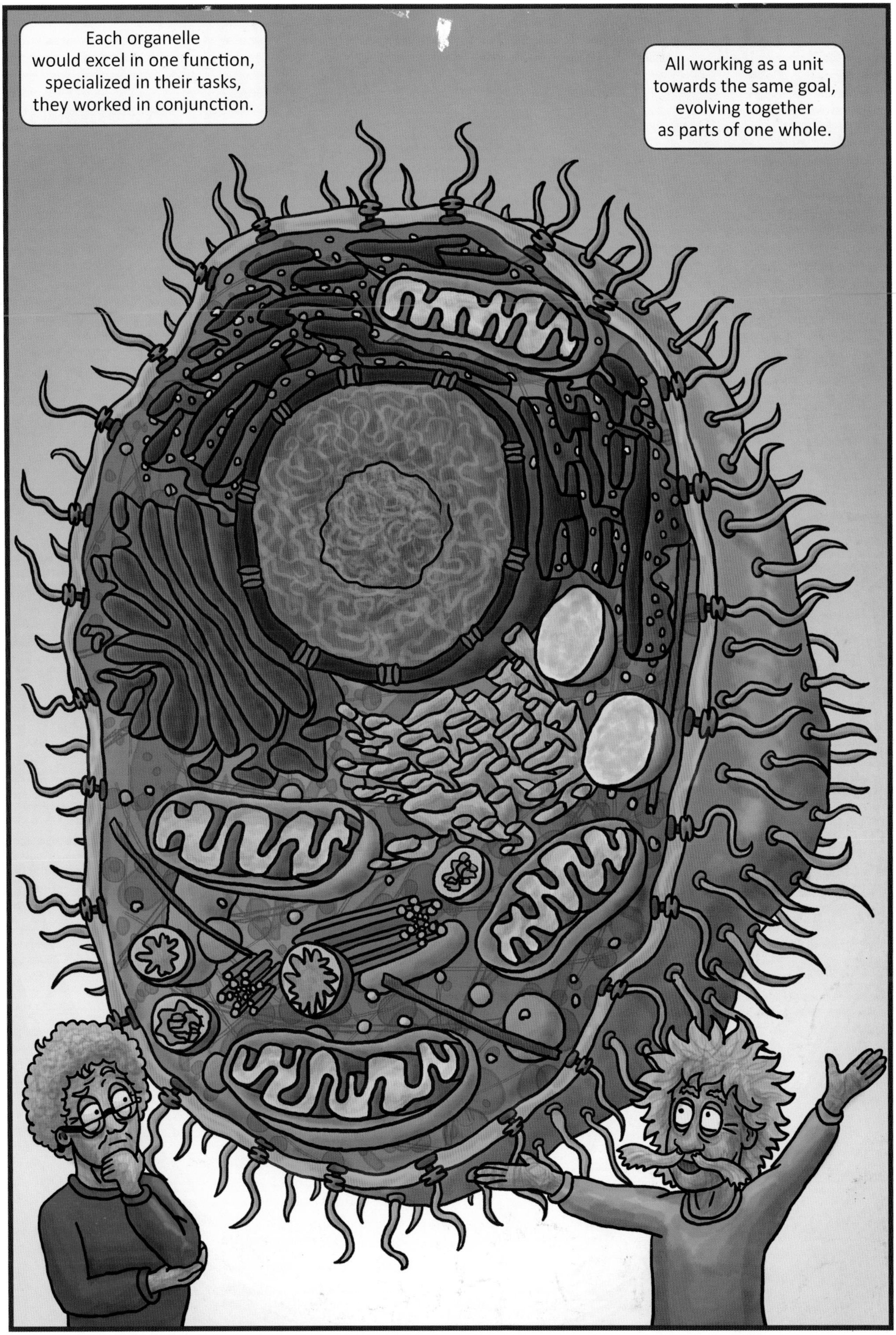

Each organelle
would excel in one function,
specialized in their tasks,
they worked in conjunction.
All working as a unit
towards the same goal,
evolving together
as parts of one whole.

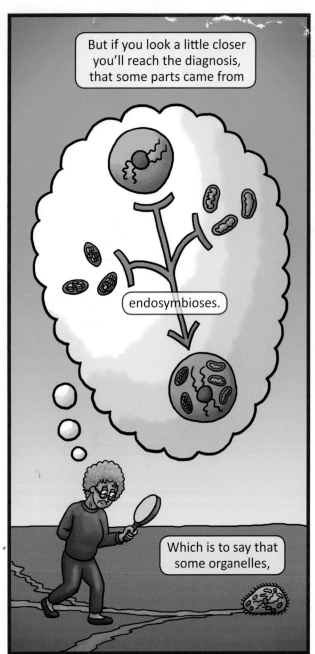

But if you look a little closer you'll reach the diagnosis, that some parts came from

endosymbioses.

Which is to say that some organelles,

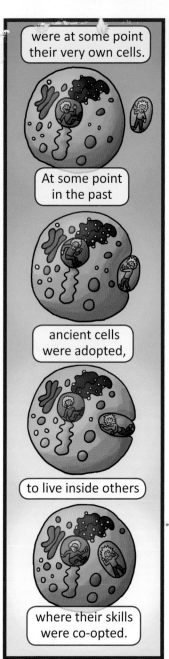

were at some point their very own cells.

At some point in the past

ancient cells were adopted,

to live inside others

where their skills were co-opted.

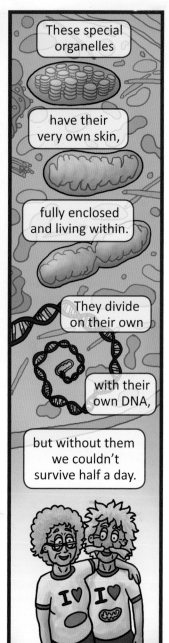

These special organelles

have their very own skin,

fully enclosed and living within.

They divide on their own

with their own DNA,

but without them we couldn't survive half a day.

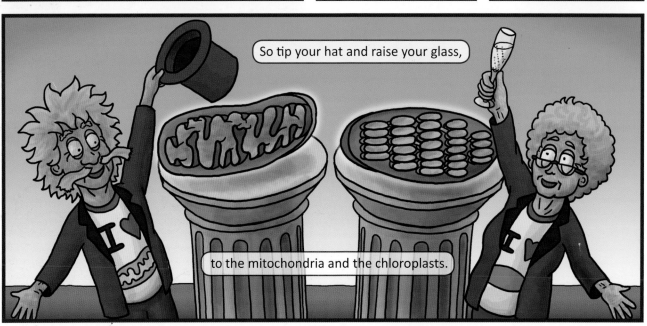

So tip your hat and raise your glass,

to the mitochondria and the chloroplasts.

Plants got chloroplasts
to grab the sun's glow,
and use that energy to make food grow.
Sadly, as animals, we don't get the same deal.
instead we are made to move for each meal.
It was at this point that we'd come to depend,
on a little bit of help from a tiny new friend.
A mitochondrion works like a small power station,
feed it some food for power generation,
that's wonderfully useful
for transportation,
protein production,
or procreation.

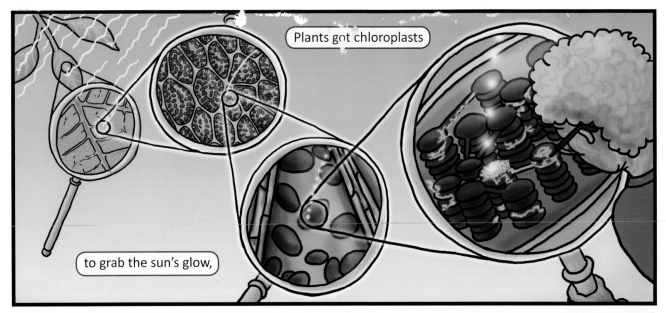

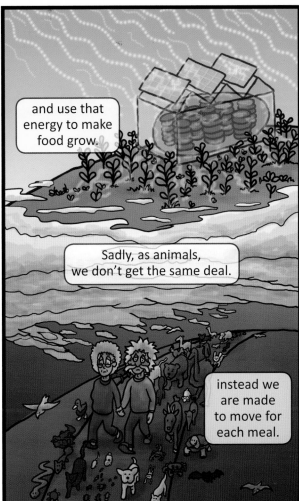

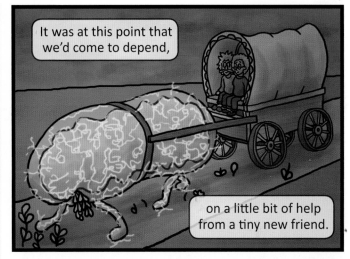

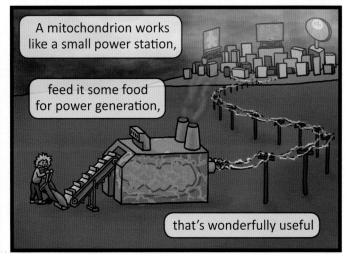

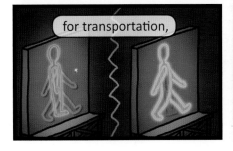

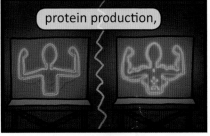

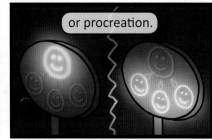

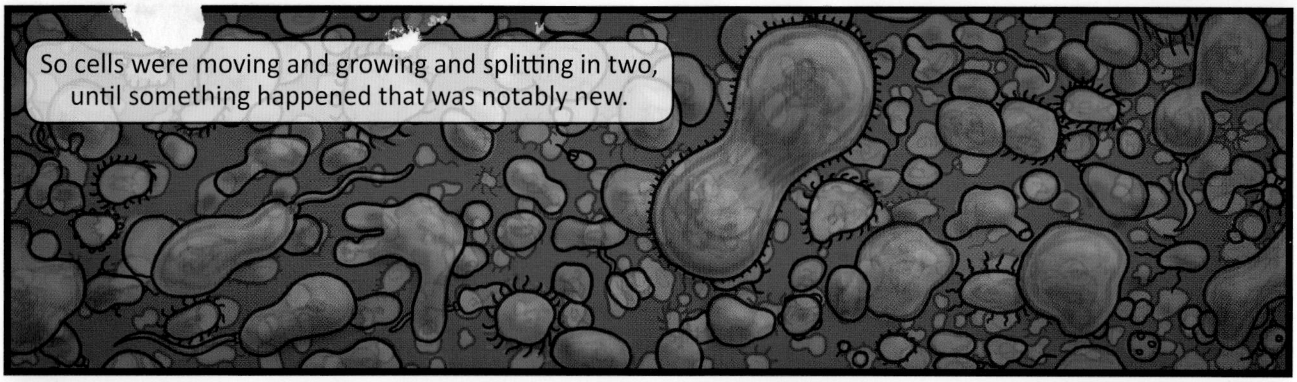
So cells were moving and growing and splitting in two,
until something happened that was notably new.

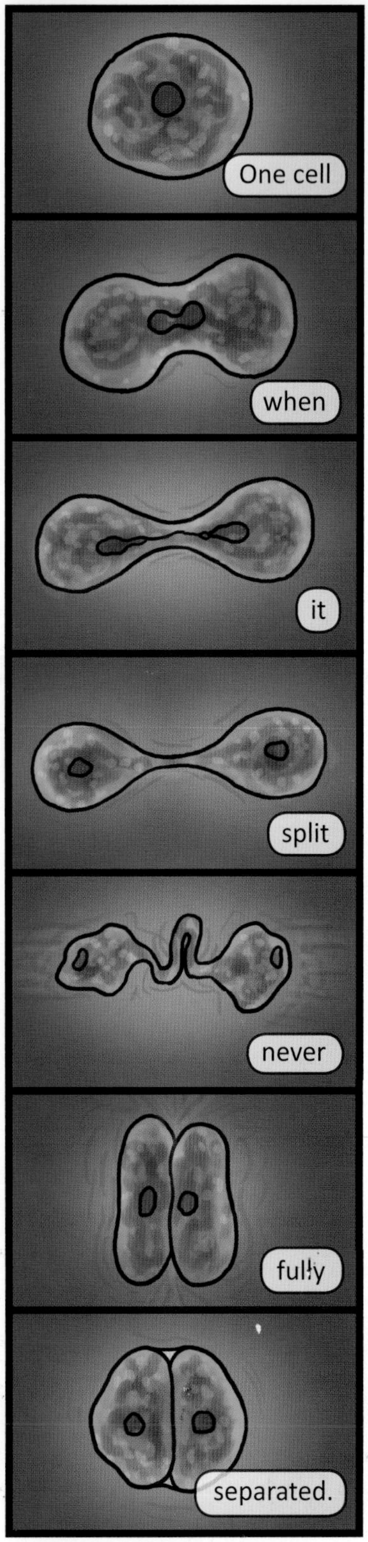
One cell
when
it
split
never
fully
separated.

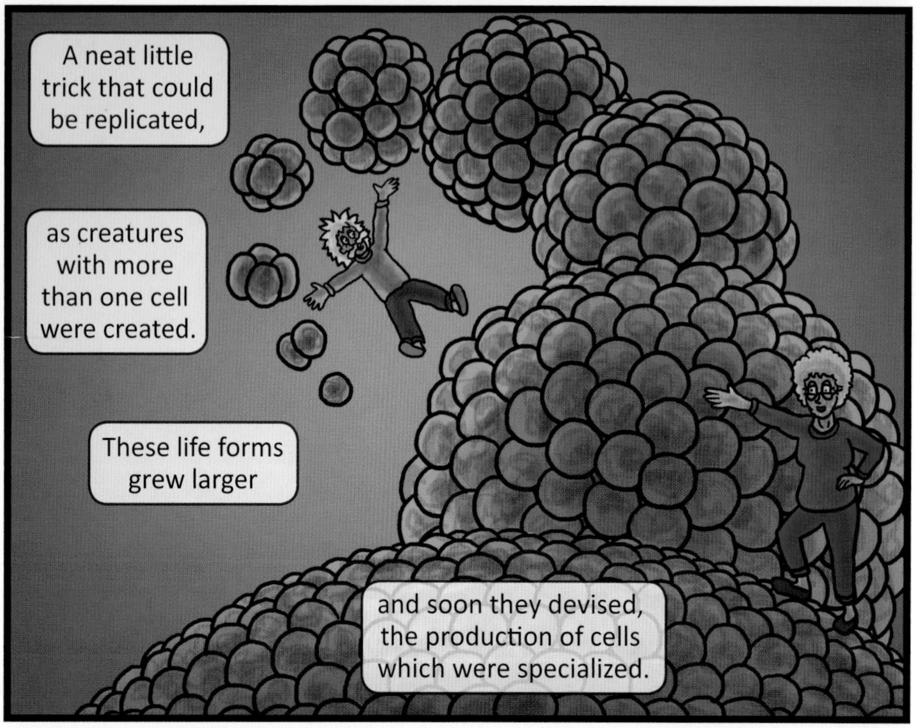
A neat little trick that could be replicated,
as creatures with more than one cell were created.
These life forms grew larger
and soon they devised, the production of cells which were specialized.

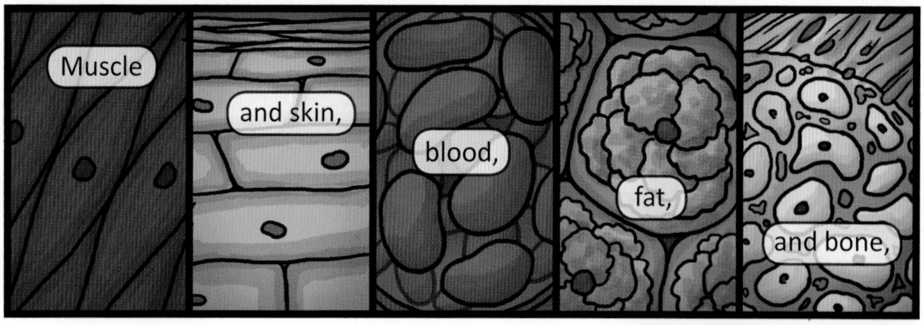
Muscle
and skin,
blood,
fat,
and bone,

all special cells with a purpose their own,
each one produced in the right body zone.
Great groups of cells would grow to comprise
tissues and organs of significant size,

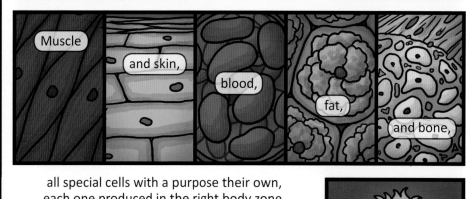

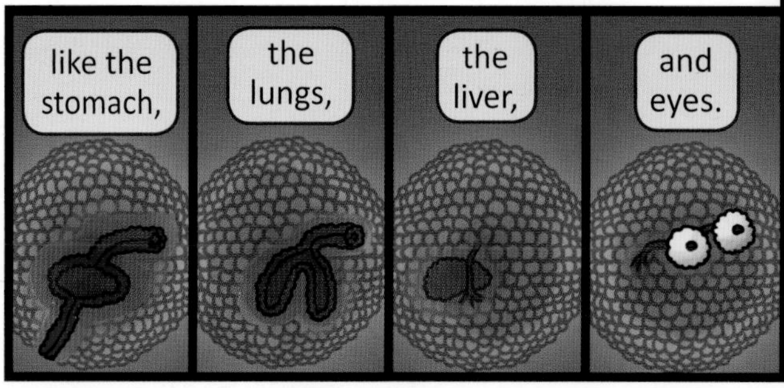
like the stomach,
the lungs,
the liver,
and eyes.

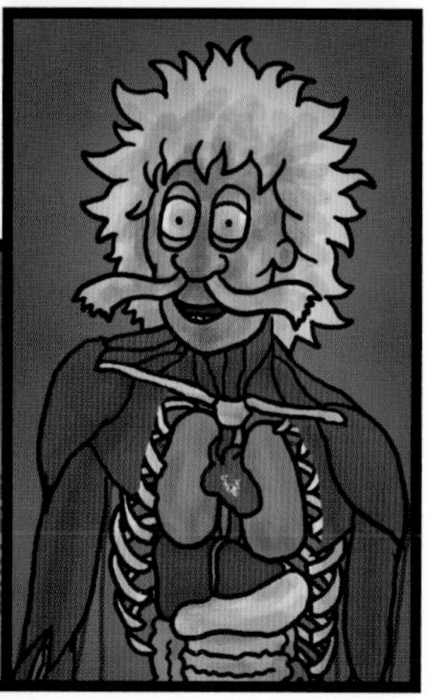

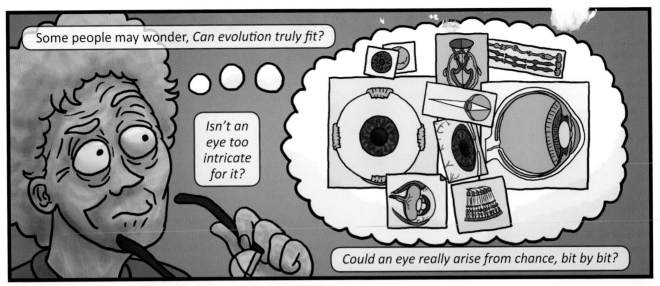

Some people may wonder, *Can evolution truly fit?*

Isn't an eye too intricate for it?

Could an eye really arise from chance, bit by bit?

But in the land

of the blind,

the one-eyed is king,

no matter how poor its light-sensing thing.

A little ain't great, but it's better than none,

with very simple eyes, survival was won.

Just one little cell

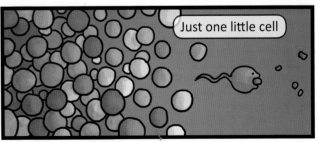

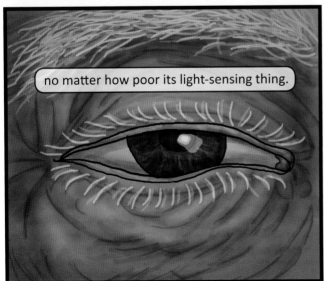

with some photo reception,

could provide the first step

towards further perception.

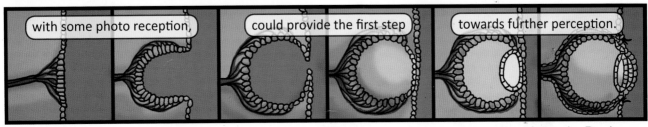

James Lu Dunbar

And it wasn't just sight, it was smell, taste, and touch,

the ability to hear, orientation and such.

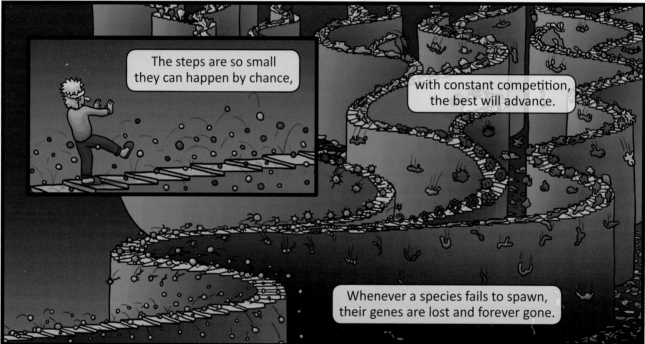

The steps are so small they can happen by chance,

with constant competition, the best will advance.

Whenever a species fails to spawn, their genes are lost and forever gone.

Lucky for us, there's been enough verve

for life to go leaping

up a living learning curve,

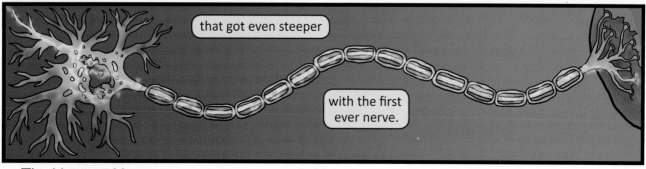

that got even steeper

with the first ever nerve.

A special new tissue like electric wire,

it takes cell signaling from a slow sloppy mire,

to a speed of relay that is magnitudes higher.

For big creatures to move, these nerves must be used,

and over time they improved and some fused.

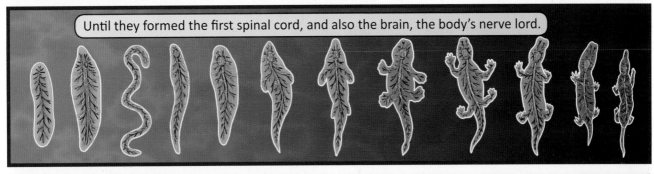

Until they formed the first spinal cord, and also the brain, the body's nerve lord.

Here data from senses could be centrally stored,

as the brain made memories to save and record.

James Lu Dunbar

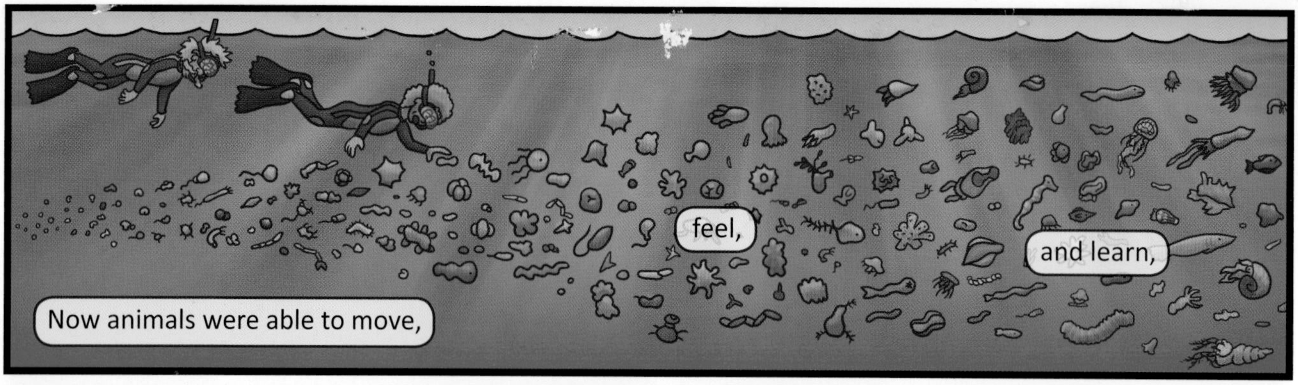
Now animals were able to move,
feel,
and learn,

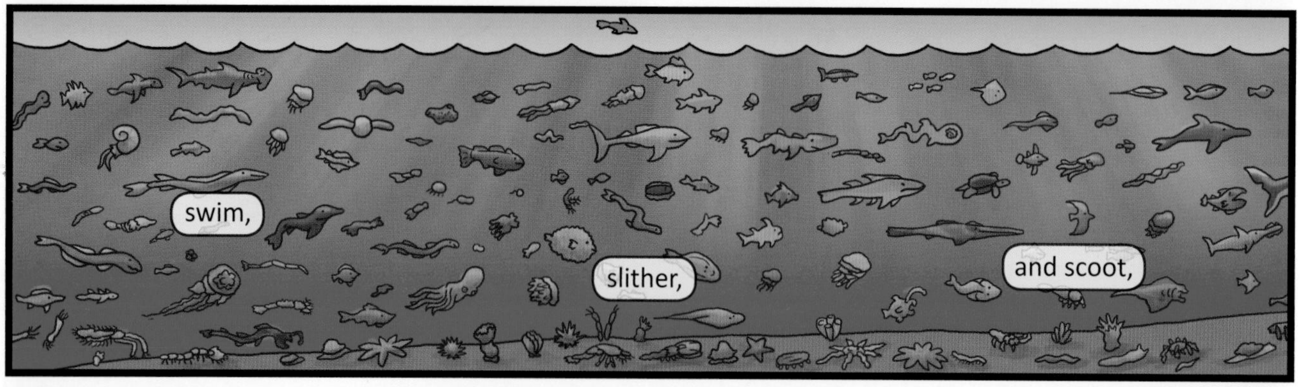
swim,
slither,
and scoot,

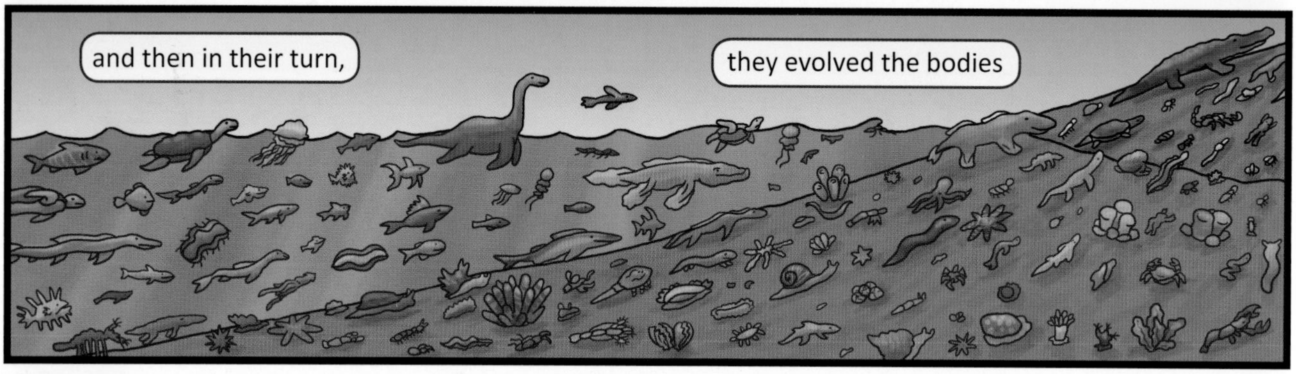
and then in their turn,
they evolved the bodies

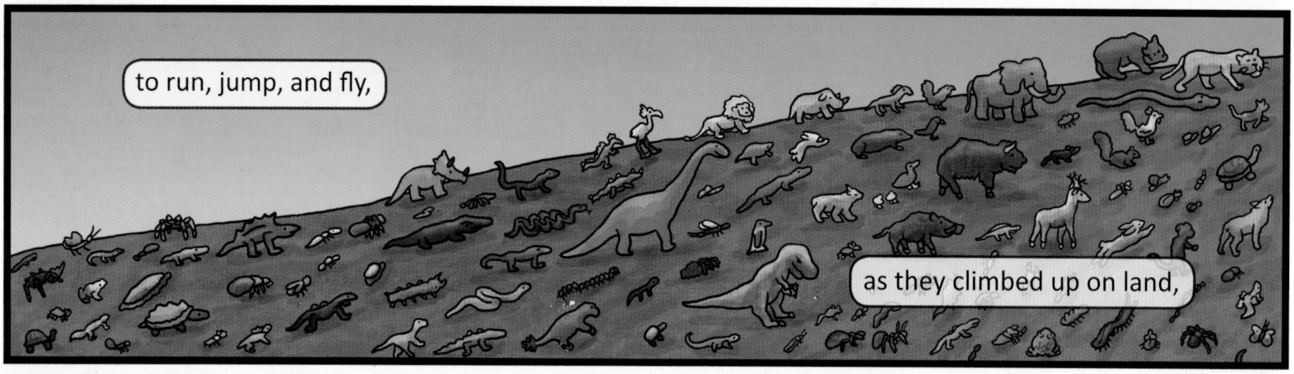
to run, jump, and fly,
as they climbed up on land,

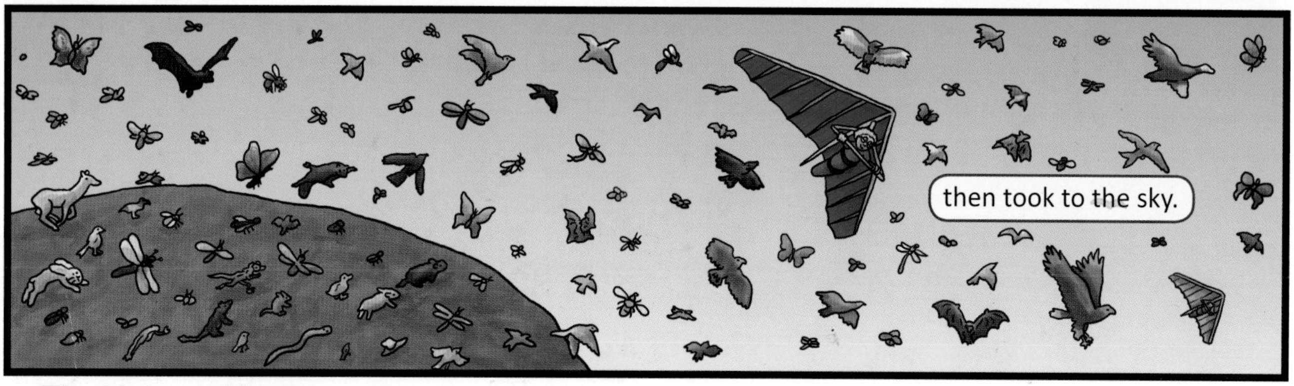
then took to the sky.

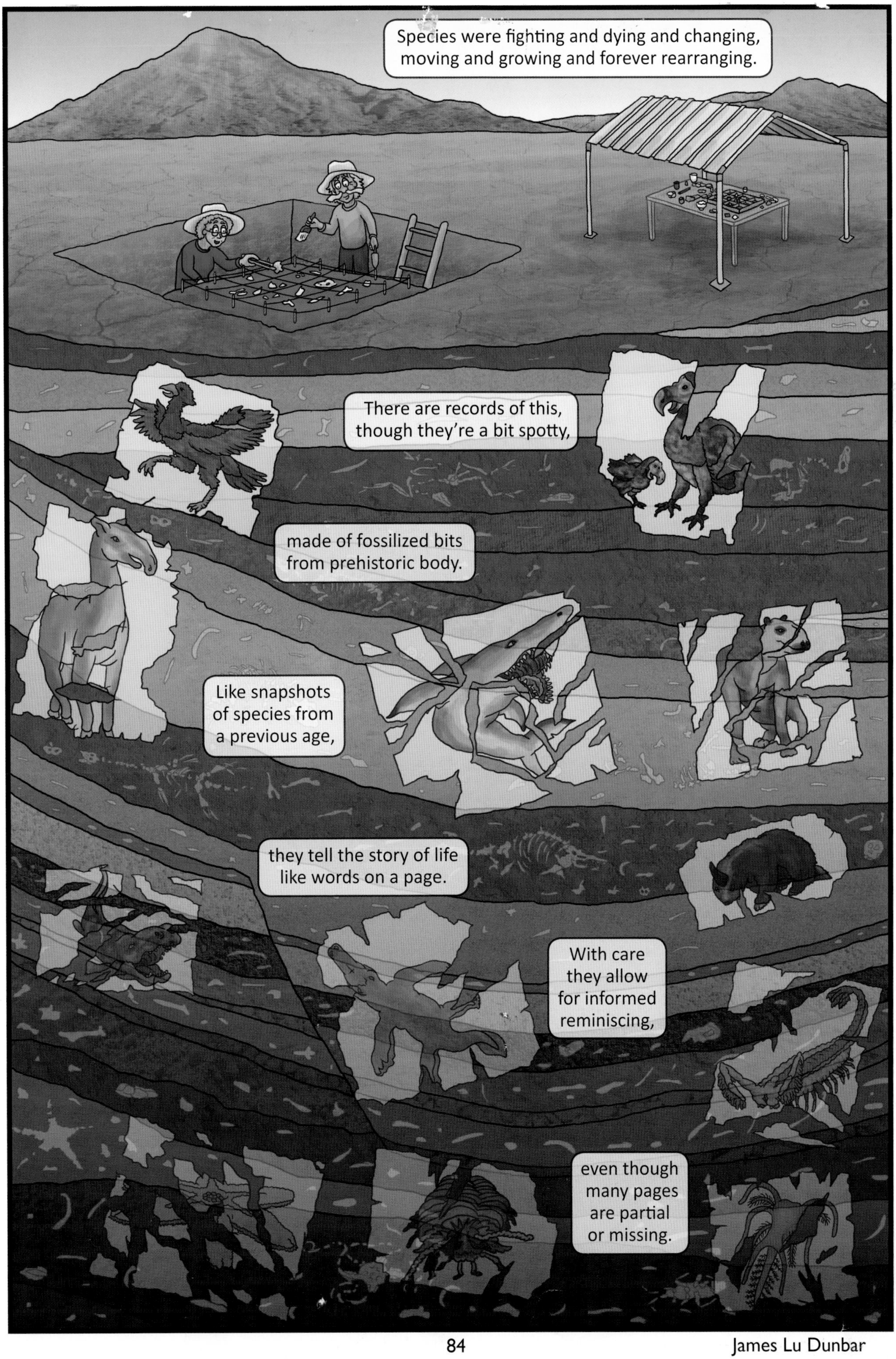
Species were fighting and dying and changing,
moving and growing and forever rearranging.
There are records of this,
though they're a bit spotty,
made of fossilized bits
from prehistoric body.
Like snapshots
of species from
a previous age,
they tell the story of life
like words on a page.
With care
they allow
for informed
reminiscing,
even though
many pages
are partial
or missing.

Through the counting of fossils

and the keeping of score,

we know five big extinctions

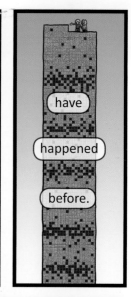

have

happened

before.

It's the most recent one that we're going to explore,

as it ended the reign of the great dinosaur.

Now mammals had evolved, just a few here and there,

but they were tiny and timid and easy to scare.

So long as the dinosaurs

were walking

around,

mammals hid up in trees or in holes underground.

Then a meteor came from out of the sky,

it crashed into Earth and made the dinosaurs die.

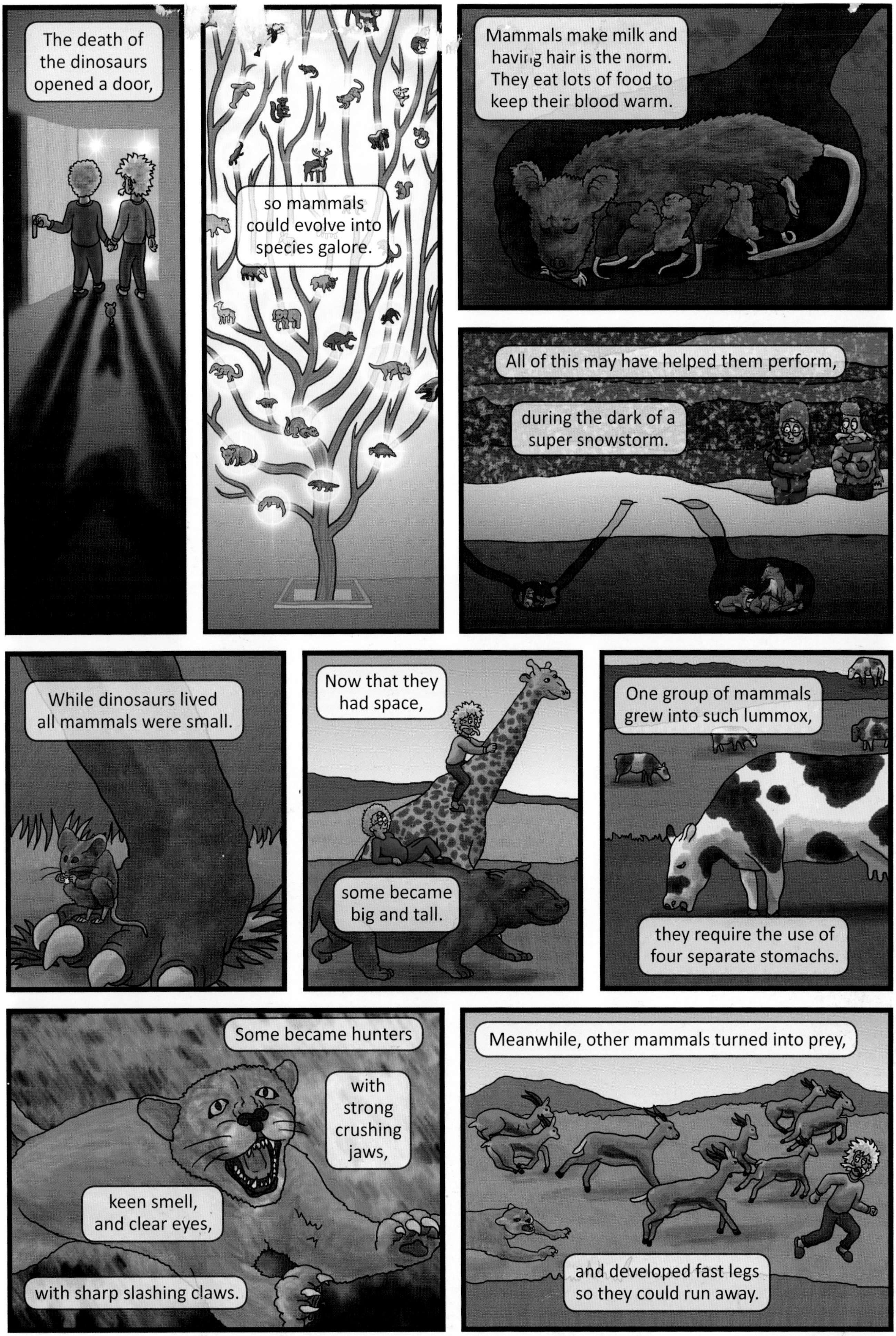

The death of the dinosaurs opened a door,
so mammals could evolve into species galore.
Mammals make milk and having hair is the norm. They eat lots of food to keep their blood warm.
All of this may have helped them perform,
during the dark of a super snowstorm.
While dinosaurs lived all mammals were small.
Now that they had space,
some became big and tall.
One group of mammals grew into such lummox,
they require the use of four separate stomachs.
Some became hunters
with strong crushing jaws,
keen smell, and clear eyes,
with sharp slashing claws.
Meanwhile, other mammals turned into prey,
and developed fast legs so they could run away.

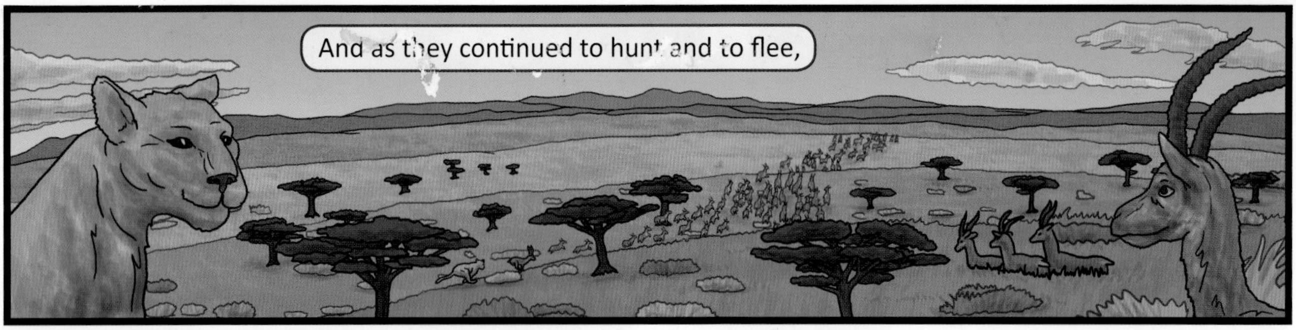
And as they continued to hunt and to flee,

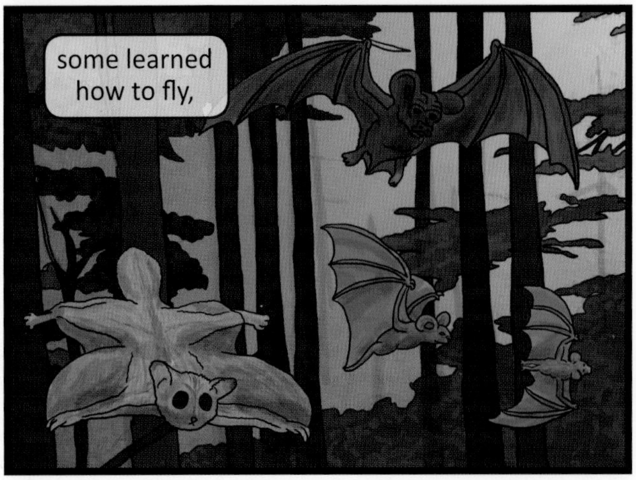
some learned how to fly,

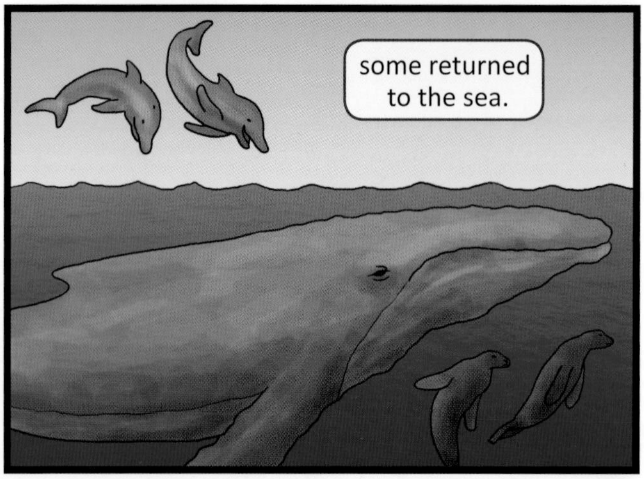
some returned to the sea.

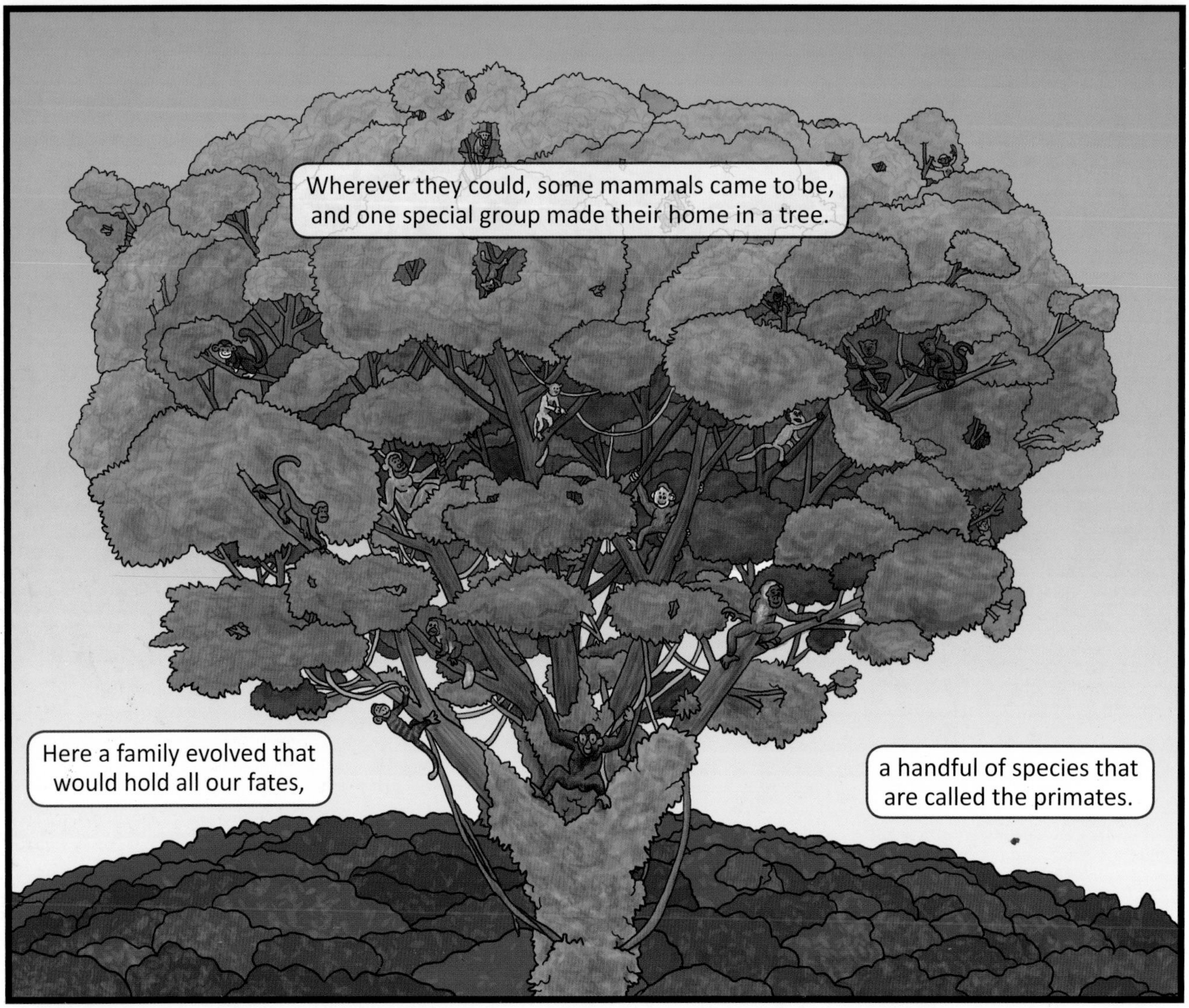
Wherever they could, some mammals came to be,
and one special group made their home in a tree.
Here a family evolved that would hold all our fates,
a handful of species that are called the primates.

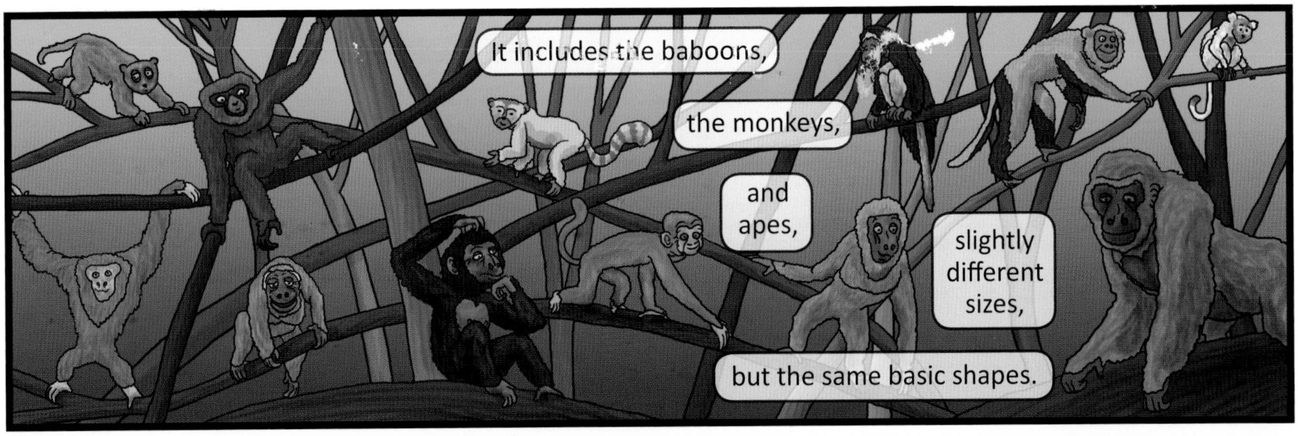
It includes the baboons,
the monkeys,
and apes,
slightly different sizes,
but the same basic shapes.

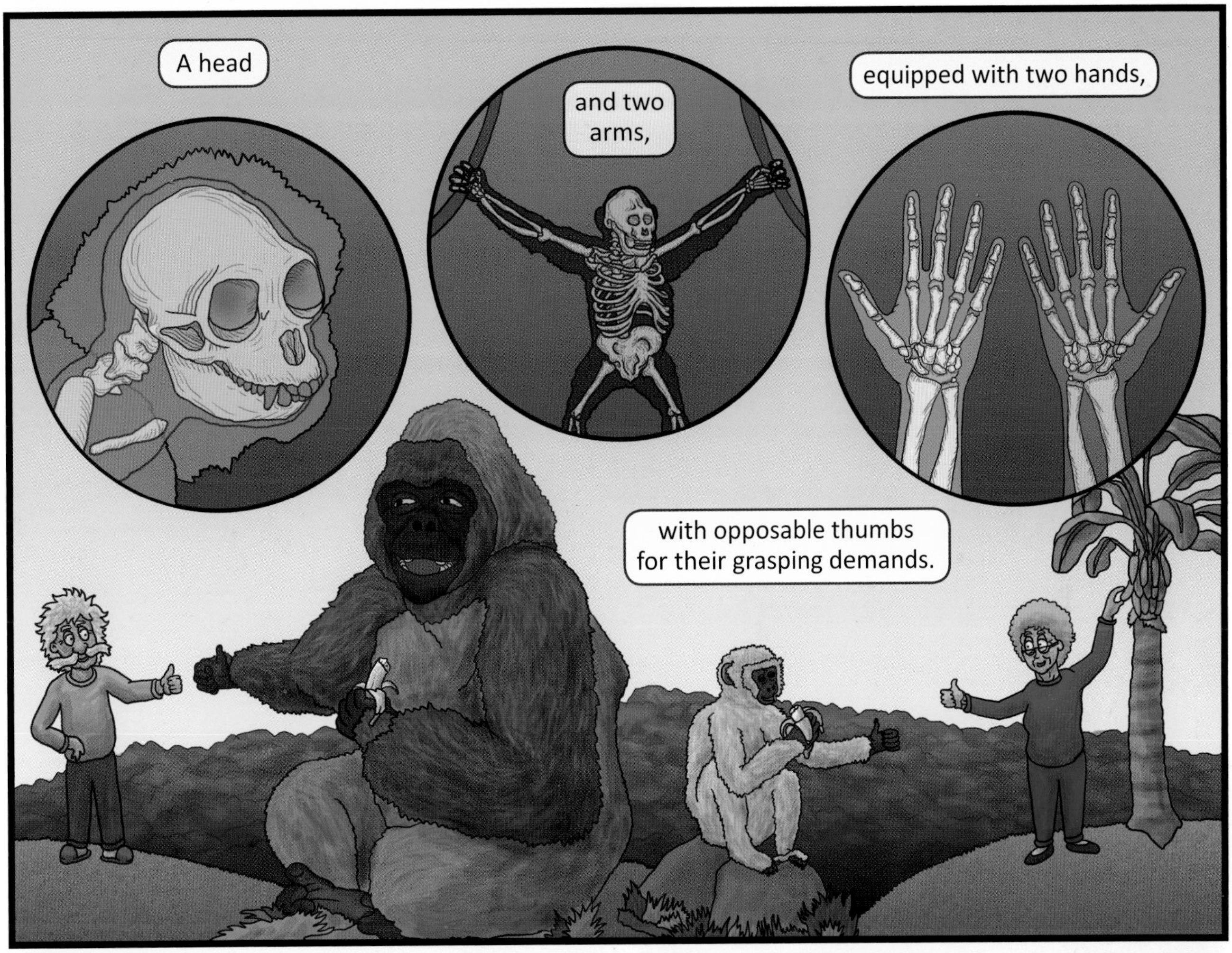
A head
and two arms,
equipped with two hands,
with opposable thumbs for their grasping demands.

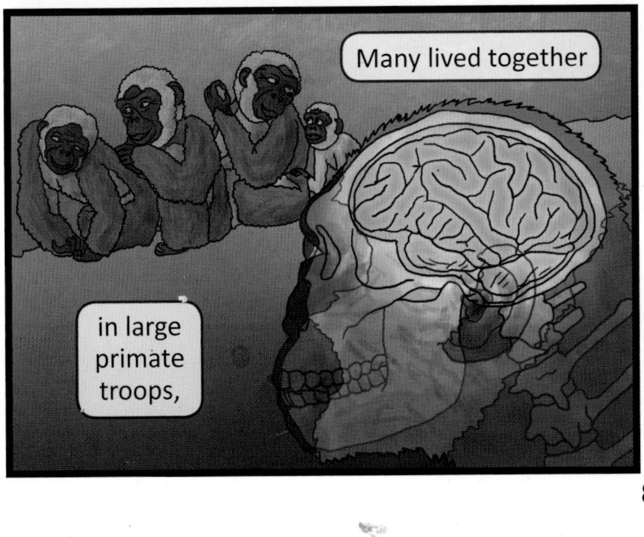
Many lived together
in large primate troops,

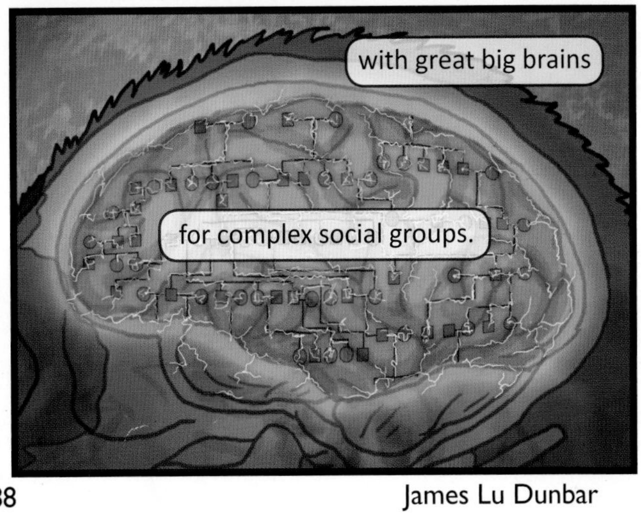
with great big brains
for complex social groups.

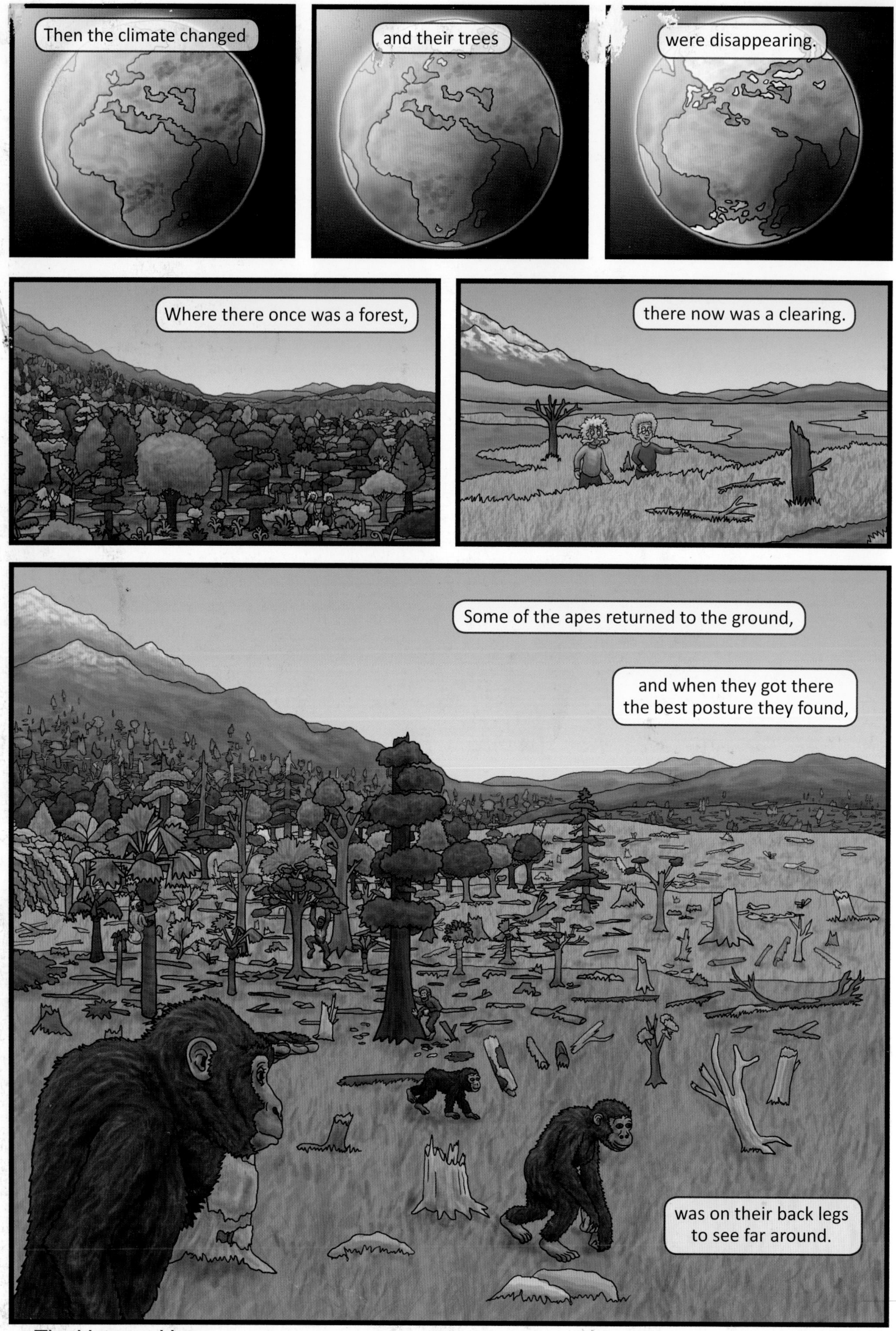
Then the climate changed
and their trees
were disappearing.
Where there once was a forest,
there now was a clearing.
Some of the apes returned to the ground,
and when they got there the best posture they found,
was on their back legs to see far around.

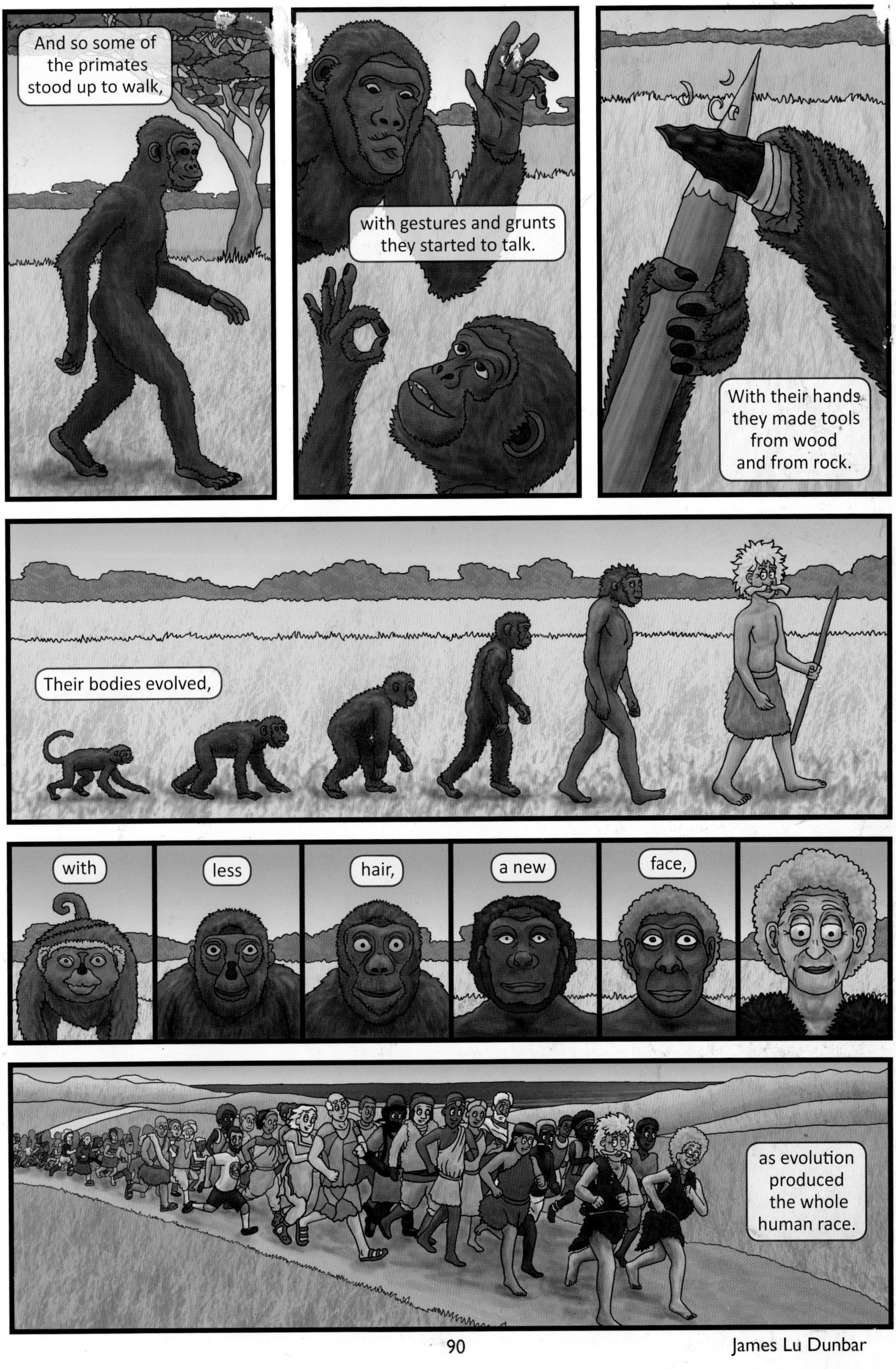
And so some of the primates stood up to walk,
with gestures and grunts they started to talk.
With their hands they made tools from wood and from rock.
Their bodies evolved,
with
less
hair,
a new
face,
as evolution produced the whole human race.

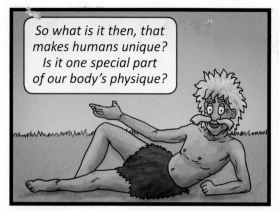

So what is it then, that makes humans unique? Is it one special part of our body's physique?

No, the feature we have that's of greatest concern, is the extent to which we are driven to learn.

Our ability to walk?

Our desire to speak?

Most animal behaviors take a while to evolve,

over many generations new instincts resolve.

But human evolution has slowly acquired,

a brain that is ready to be rapidly rewired,

with novel new skills that may be required.

We probe and we play,

we engage and explore,

we listen and look, and learn a little more.

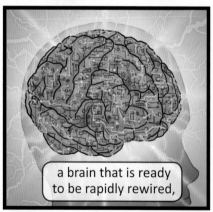

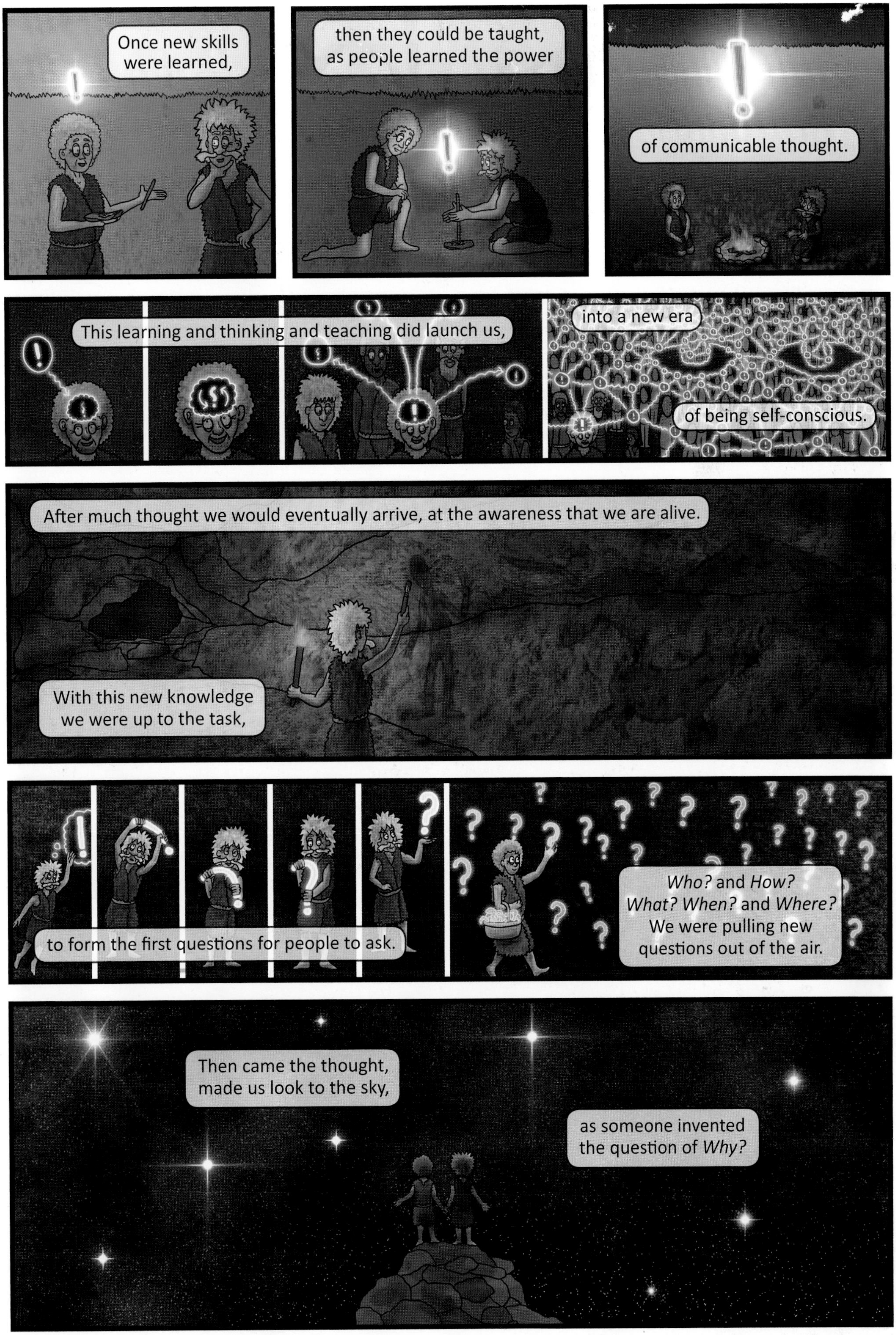

Once new skills were learned,
then they could be taught, as people learned the power
of communicable thought.
This learning and thinking and teaching did launch us,
into a new era
of being self-conscious.
After much thought we would eventually arrive, at the awareness that we are alive.
With this new knowledge we were up to the task,
to form the first questions for people to ask.
Who? and *How?* *What? When?* and *Where?* We were pulling new questions out of the air.
Then came the thought, made us look to the sky,
as someone invented the question of *Why?*

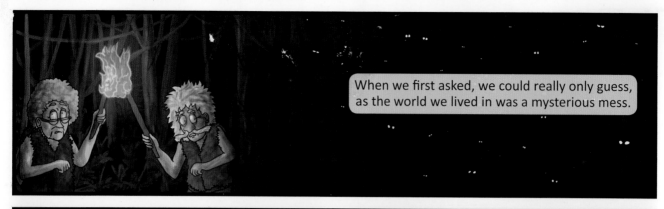

When we first asked, we could really only guess,
as the world we lived in was a mysterious mess.

But as our questions would come to surround us,
they helped us to learn of the world around us,

whose wild workings used to confound us.

We learned to raise crops

and domesticate beasts,

control mighty fire,

and cultivate yeasts,

as agriculture made for bountiful feasts.

The need to find food was slowly withdrawn,

as an agrarian age was starting to dawn.

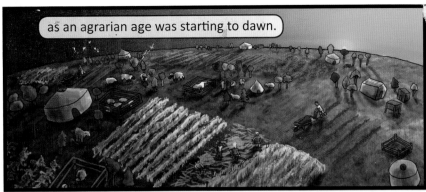

A farmer is able to feed some of his neighbors,

who each specialize

in their own

set of labors.

Each in their field can gain expertise,

trading their goods through a system of fees.

Great groups could now flourish in fertile locations

creating and collecting amazing accumulations,

forming the foundation

for civilizations.

As societies grew larger

and more complicated,

new needs for new skills were being created.

94

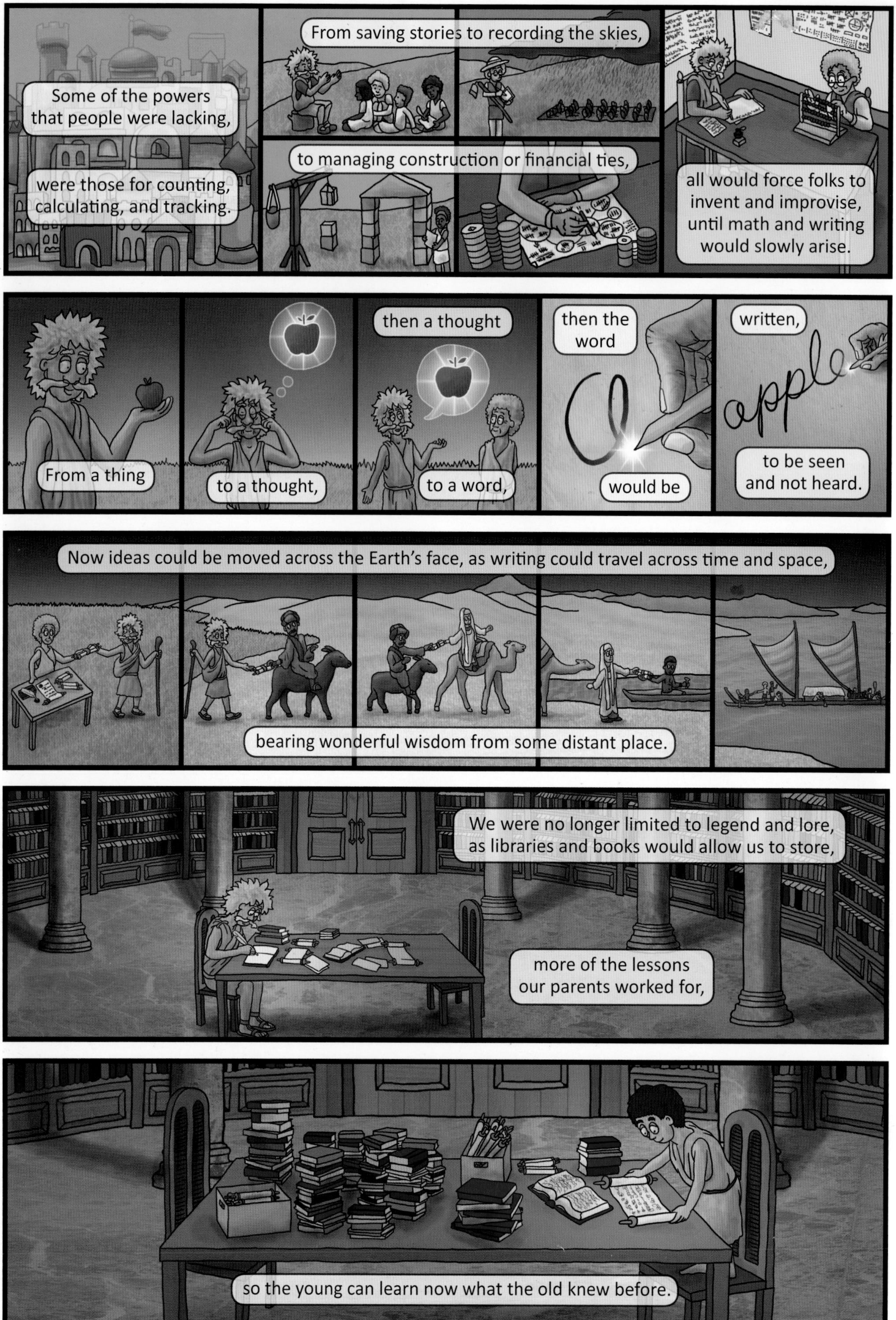
Some of the powers that people were lacking,
were those for counting, calculating, and tracking.
From saving stories to recording the skies,
to managing construction or financial ties,
all would force folks to invent and improvise, until math and writing would slowly arise.
From a thing
to a thought,
then a thought
to a word,
then the word
would be
written,
apple
to be seen and not heard.
Now ideas could be moved across the Earth's face, as writing could travel across time and space,
bearing wonderful wisdom from some distant place.
We were no longer limited to legend and lore, as libraries and books would allow us to store,
more of the lessons our parents worked for,
so the young can learn now what the old knew before.

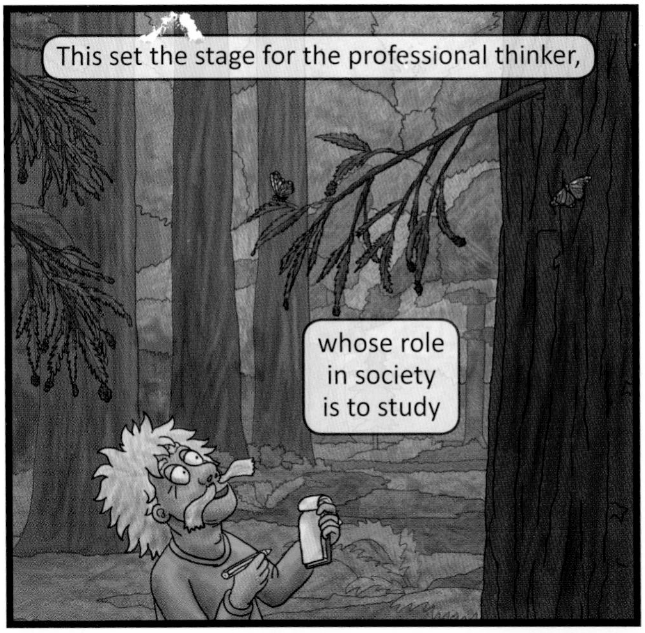
This set the stage for the professional thinker,
whose role in society is to study

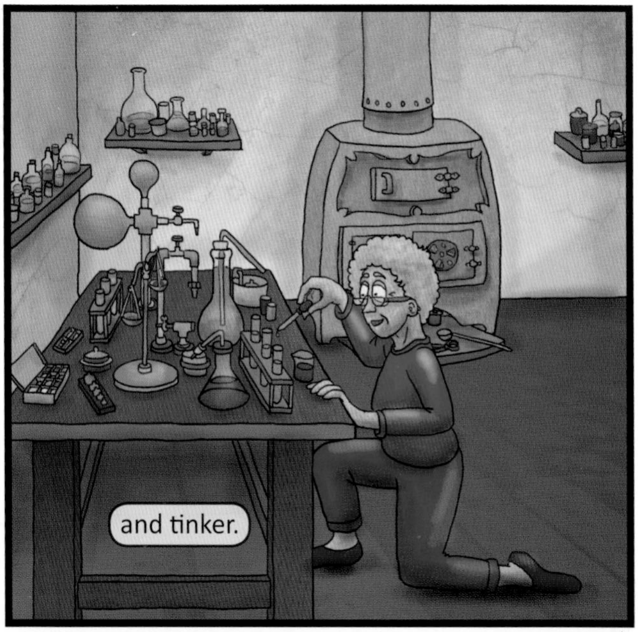
and tinker.

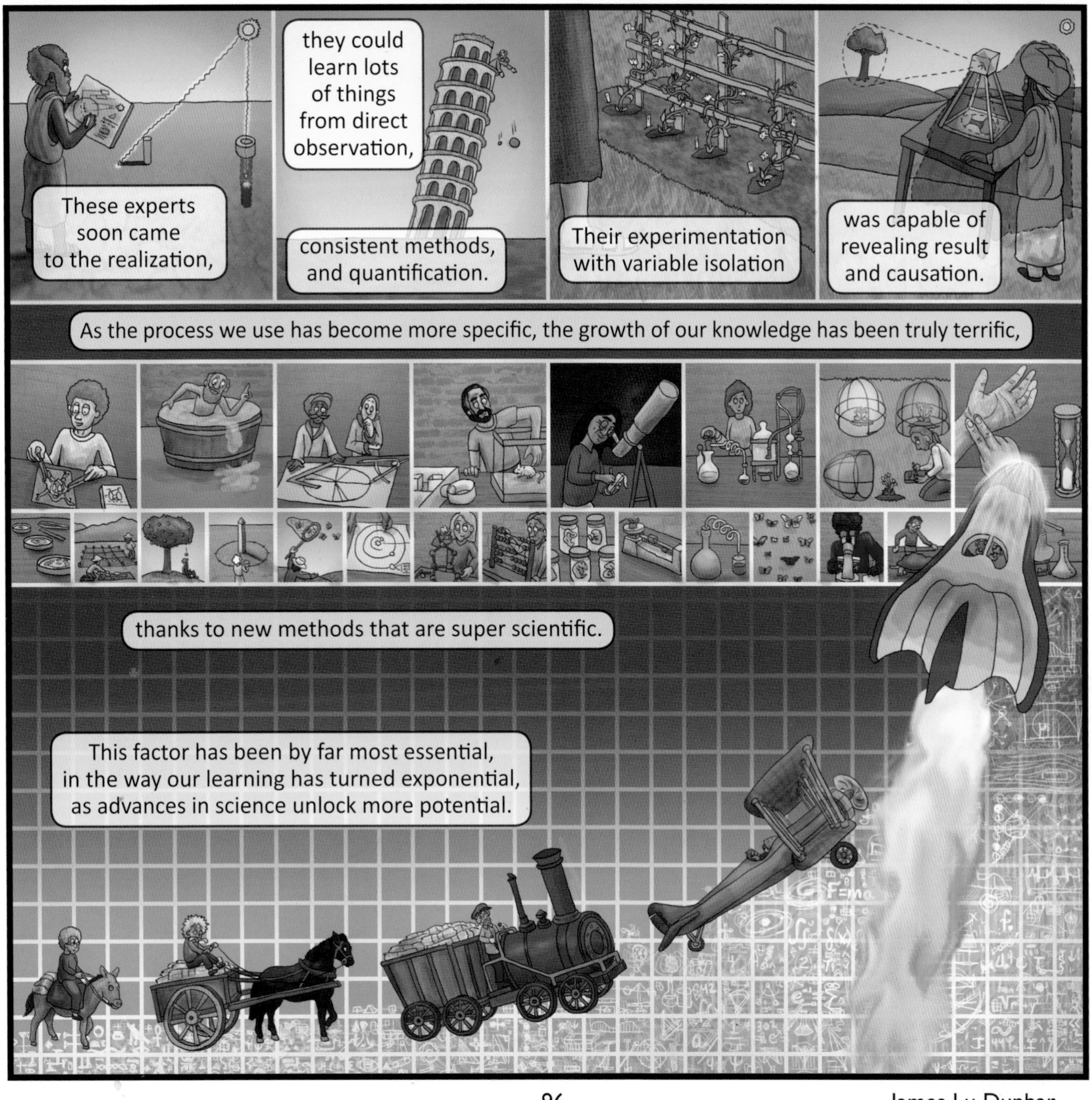
These experts soon came to the realization,
they could learn lots of things from direct observation,
consistent methods, and quantification.
Their experimentation with variable isolation
was capable of revealing result and causation.
As the process we use has become more specific, the growth of our knowledge has been truly terrific,
thanks to new methods that are super scientific.
This factor has been by far most essential, in the way our learning has turned exponential, as advances in science unlock more potential.

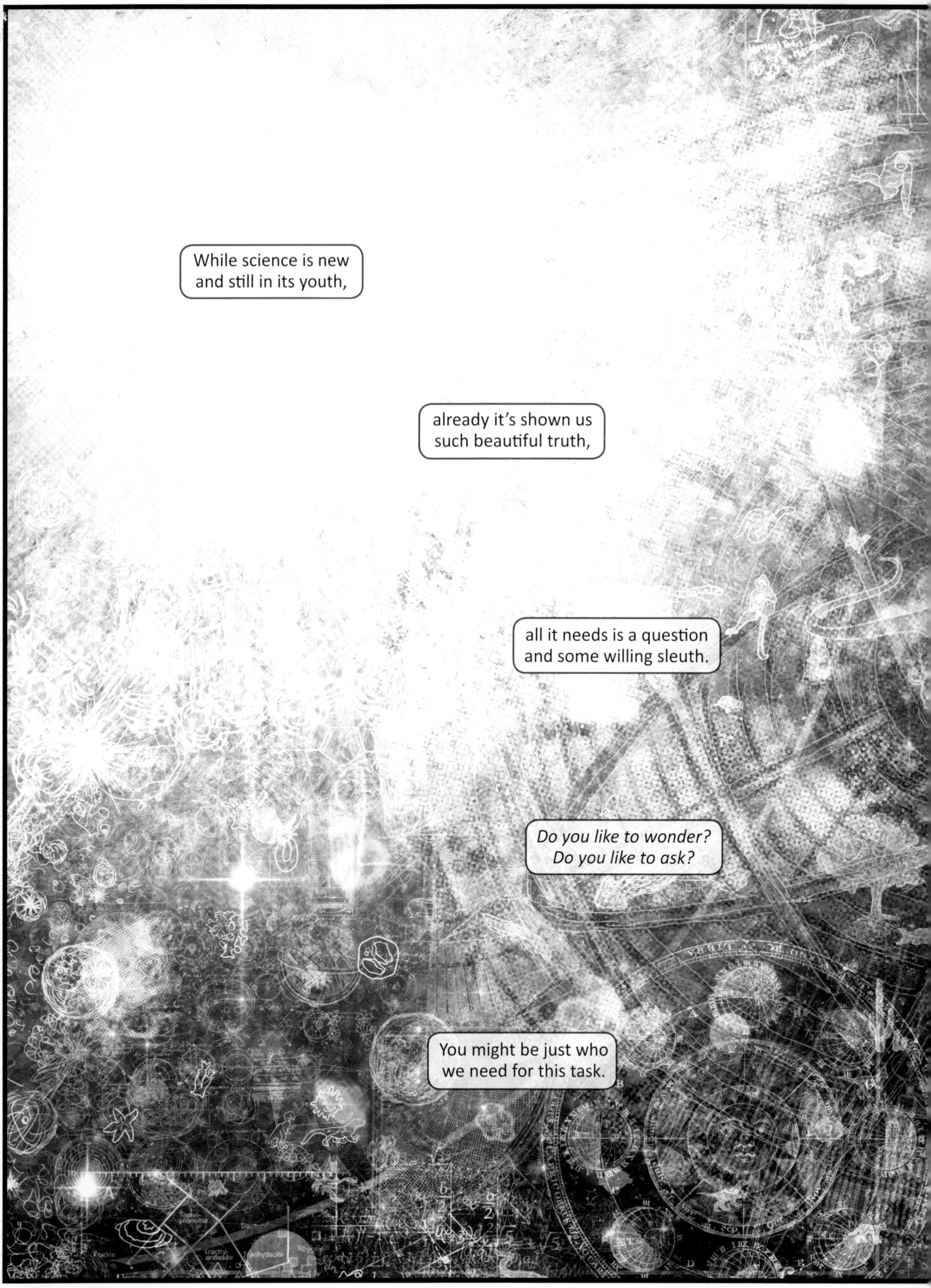
While science is new and still in its youth,
already it's shown us such beautiful truth,
all it needs is a question and some willing sleuth.
Do you like to wonder? Do you like to ask?
You might be just who we need for this task.

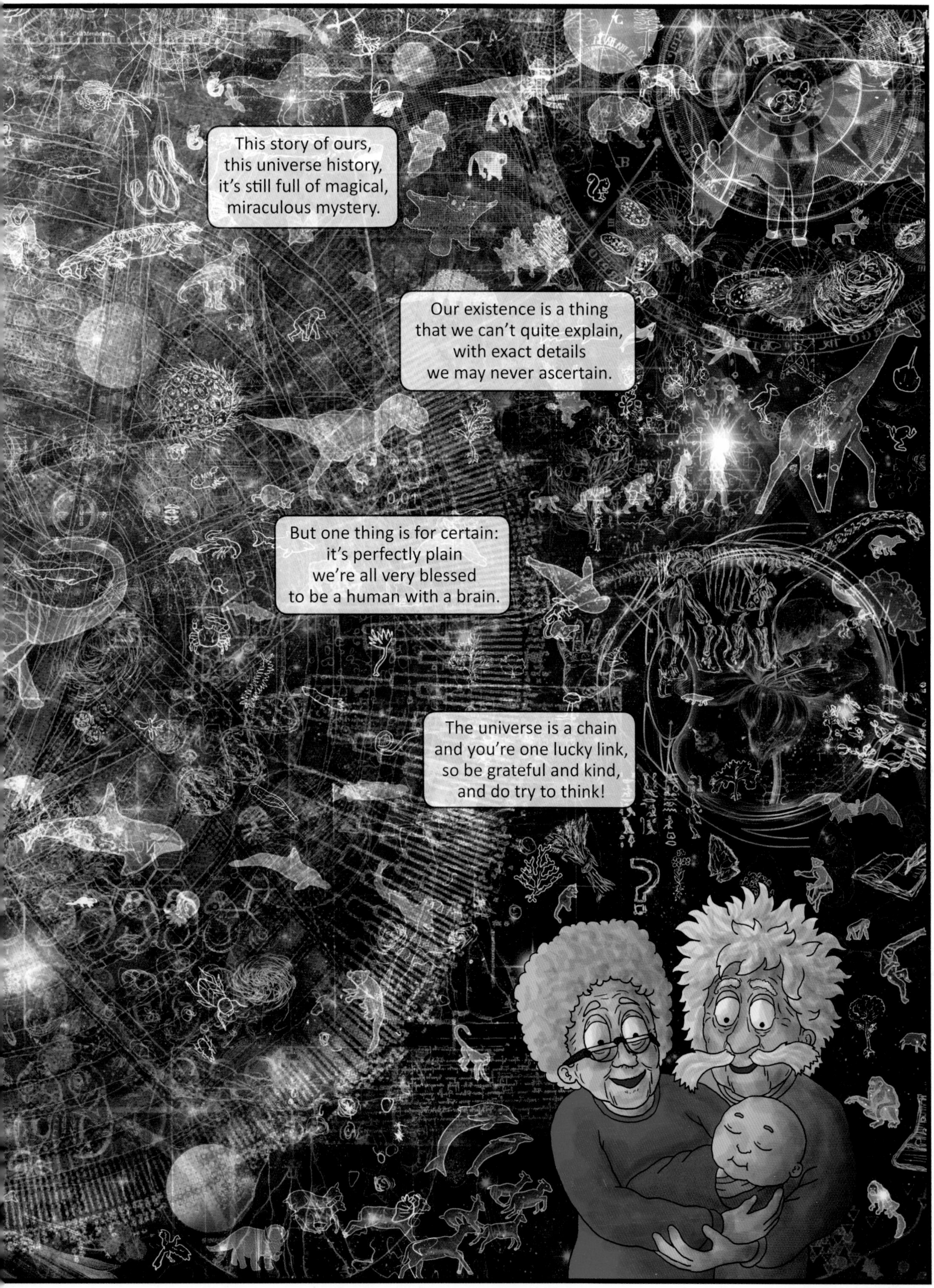
This story of ours,
this universe history,
it's still full of magical,
miraculous mystery.
Our existence is a thing
that we can't quite explain,
with exact details
we may never ascertain.
But one thing is for certain:
it's perfectly plain
we're all very blessed
to be a human with a brain.
The universe is a chain
and you're one lucky link,
so be grateful and kind,
and do try to think!

This book would not have been possible without Kickstarter.com and the generous support of over 350 gracious backers. Many thanks to all of you, I truly appreciate all of your assistance.

Extra special thanks to the following family, friends and fans:
Trina; Mimi Lou, Lukas, Teo & Andris Skuja; Ian & Kelly Dunbar; Dana & Jim Jones;
Margaret Lou, Steve, Mia, Maggie & Nic McDermott; William, Debbie & Wes Lou; Pau Pau;
Ryan Clark & Molly Jones; Grannie & Jim Dunbar; Annie & Howard Jones;
Isaac & Becca Wilcox, Janice & Zeke Chapler; Zach, Swapna & Riya Zinn; Kirk, Joan,
Nadia & Vanja; Ben Gordon; Miriam Walter, Alex DiGiorgio & Izzy; John Hillman; Leah & Justin;
Matt, Gary & Janice St. Peter; The Granberg Training Center; Matt Zaldivar; Ginger Campbell;
Branko Kolvek & Lois Saldana; The Oshun Family; Scott & Sruthi; Stoci Thomsen;
Sheri Glucoft Wong, Jessie, Steven & Avra; Patrick Hamilton & Violet Lehrer; Miranda Gabriel;
Nina Frank & Paul Manzi; Lindsay Barrick & Jerry Talkington; Dave & Jessie Hahn;
Megan DeLong & Erich Eilenberger; Wilfred U. Codrington III; DaddyChurchill; Nick Rosenthal;
Kaylena Bray; Cynthia Stokes Brown; The Barnes Street Society of Gentlemen Scholars;
Jenny Gold; Frances Dauster; The Ten Ten; Matthew Reagan; Barry Dow; Boys Night;
Marc Neulight; Stephen Lemelin; The Hirst Family; Alejandra Zinn; Katelin & Nnamdi Etoh;
Sheila Sondik & Paul Sarvasy; Ian Warthin; Magnus Hollmo; Genny Hoffman; Elliot Waring;
Stella Klemperer; Steve Atlas; Julia Hawes; Anna Fedman; Christine Okike;
Arianna Cassidy & Matt Bald; Caitlin O'Connell; Grantland Gears; Evan Hammer;
Michelle & Nigel; Amanda Wight; Lisette Caissie & Jason Luchtefeld; Brandy D. Ellis;
The Usie Family; Gloria Charles; William Matthew & Nora Ellen Scott; The Schumakers;
Brian, Susyn, Ethan & Megan; Tony Roberts; S. Alan Coffman; Kelly Mullins; Ronald Gotong;
Genevieve & Marielle; Caroline Randa; Michael & Jeanie Strong; Wolfie; Steven Scott Bardone;
Timothy Wascoe; Oliver D. Dickerson III; Bob Hillier, Red Pine Observatory, Canada;
Sydney & Troy Wilson; Black Pine Circle, Berkeley High & Brown University;
Lorcan & Griff Brondum; Melanie & Emily Hsu; Olivia Michele Konsavage; The Solomon Family;
David Walter Niederauer; Joey, Jackie & Ellie Dowling; Terence, Clare & Aeryn Chua;
Bear Aneurin Jones; Raechel, Jonathan & Zachary; Michaela & Liam Lynch; Will Nourse;
Marivi Lerdo de Tejada; Joseph DeBarr; Marian Herenius; The Melissa E Lucarelli Family;
The Snyder Family; Pam & Steve Solomon; Bernard & Elsa; Rex G. Mitchell & Family;
Cassidy Ruth de la Peña; Ms. Jessie and Mr. Ben, Classroom El Morado 2013-14;
Scott & Kyra Gray; Monica Vaughan; Rica Sirbaugh French; Erik Roberto Serna; Gord Walpole;
The Wetzel Family of Cincinnati OH; Adam Grandt; Alexander & Elena Pavlides; Krista Hoxie;
Steven Hosford; The Peteks; Cora & Fiona; The Grandparents of Sophia Louise Allan;
Paul Dale; Bruce W. Casey; Nancy Agland; Julie Palais; Bhupinder Randhawa.

A Note from the Author

I am not a professional scientist, just an enthusiastic amateur with a library card.

I was able to write this book because of countless people who have
devoted their lives to furthering the scientific knowledge of the human race.
As a result of their hard work we now know more about ourselves
and our place in the universe than we have ever known before,
and the rate at which we continue to learn more is only accelerating.

However, there are still plenty of mysteries when it comes to exactly
how we ended up here and where we might be going. There are still an
infinite supply of unanswered questions left. And there always will be,
because the more we know, the more questions we can ask.

There are questions about the origin of our universe, our planet, and our
ancestors, about matter and energy we cannot easily perceive, about how
things work when they're very small or large or hot or cold or dense or distant.
Questions about the operation of organic processes, from those playing out across
our planet to the ones that occur between our ears and within our cells.

Over the coming decades and centuries we will uncover answers to many
of these questions, but it is most certain that many more will remain a mystery.
We'll come up with new questions, and all along the way we'll make mistakes.
We will discover that some of our current models and assumptions are entirely
wrong or at least not entirely accurate. And not only is this acceptable,
it is necessary. It is an inevitable, integral part of this process. If we already
knew the answers it wouldn't be progress, we wouldn't be learning.

On that note, I'd like to mention that this book is far from perfect. I've poured
a huge amount of time and energy into researching, writing, editing, illustrating,
publishing, and promoting this book, but I'll be the first to admit that there's still
plenty of room for improvement. Someday I may return to this book to update
it with new information, new verse and new illustrations, so if you have any
suggestions or corrections I'd love to hear them.

And if you have a lot of suggestions, you might want to consider becoming a
scientist, or writing a book, or drawing some comics, because I bet you
would be good at it and have a great time doing it.

For additional resources please visit www.JLDunbar.com

About the Author

James "Jamie" Lu Dunbar has published two other books:
7 River Riddles and *Gordy McGranite Grapples with Gradients: A Calculus Story.*

Jamie Dunbar lives in Oakland, CA where he helps manage
the Sirius Puppy Training school, James & Kenneth Publishers and Dog Star Daily.
Jamie went to Brown University where he majored in Sociology and Visual Art,
specializing in oil painting and bookmaking. In addition to writing and illustrating,
Jamie enjoys cooking and sports and games of all sorts, and of course...
...science!